The Toddler's BUSY BOOK

MERCIER PRESS, Douglas Village, Cork
www.mercierpresss.ie

Trade enquiries to Columba Mercier Distribution,
55a Spruce Avenue, Stillorgan Industrial Park, Blackrock, Dublin

ISBN: 978 1 85635 539 1

First published in 1998 by Meadowbrook Press
This revised Irish edition first published in 2007

Mercier Press receives financial assistance from
the Arts Council / An Chomhairle Ealaíon

Printed and bound by J.H. Haynes & Co. Ltd, Sparkford

The Toddler's
BUSY
BOOK

Trish Kuffner

MERCIER PRESS

WHAT YOU NEED TO READ

Dedication

For Johanna, our toddler-in-residence.

Writing this book with you was difficult;

without you it would have been impossible.

Acknowledgements

Writing a book while homeschooling three children, chasing a toddler and struggling through the early months of pregnancy was not an easy job and I could not have done it without the help of some wonderful people.

First and foremost, I thank God for His love, mercy and grace, for His leading in my life and for the daily strength He gives me to meet the many challenges of parenting.

I sincerely thank my mother, Irene McGeorge, my mother-in-law, Betty Kuffner and my friend, Joy Francescini, who have been so willing this past year to care for my children when I have needed time to write. I am so grateful for the help you have given me.

To my husband, Wayne and our children Andria, Emily, Joshua and Johanna, I thank you for being willing to put up with grilled cheese sandwich dinners, an absence of clean clothes and Saturdays without Mom. I really appreciate the sacrifices you've all made.

Contents

Foreword

I was reading a fascinating article recently about how 'conventional or accepted wisdom' is not necessarily the truth . The irony and accuracy of this statement was borne out almost immediately to me in an email from Mary Feehan of Mercier Press. 'Mark' it went, 'would you like to do an introduction for another Trish Kuffner book?' Now here's the problem: because I'm a father of four, it was presumed I actually knew something about rearing children. This presumption led to me being asked, last year, to write a foreword to Trish Kuffner's *The Preschoolers Busy Book* (which by the way, is as vital in a house with children, as a first aid kit). I was then interviewed by several respected publications about the book, on the basis of my 'expertise'. In the meantime, my wife Audrey had rolled her eyeballs to heaven so often, she at times resembled a slot machine that was unable to stop revolving.

My point, and yes there is one, is that through a series of mistaken assumptions, the conventional wisdom now is that I have some expertise in the area of child rearing. This is a dangerous untruth (and I'm paraphrasing my wife here!). I know enough to know how little I know about those mysterious aliens I call my children. Trish Kuffner's books have taught me that there is a bottomless pit of possibilities at our fingertips to keep our children entertained and stimulated. What's great is that these are right under our noses in our own homes, and they don't cost a fortune!

Personally I find the toddler stage very difficult because I just don't understand the gurgles, hisses and squeaks that pass for toddler language; unlike my wife, for whom every goo goo, ga ga tells a thousand words. Further proof, if any was needed, that God is a woman. So, if like me, your toddler-minding skills don't extend much beyond pushing the play button on the DVD player, then you will find *The Toddler's Busy Book* even more invaluable than *The Preschooler's Busy Book*, because this age really is the crucible of your children's development and formation. At this age they are at their most absorbent and spongelike, and so it is crucial to know that what you're putting in is appropriate.

To be honest, a lot of what Trish Kuffner tells us in these books is good old-fashioned common sense and that necessity is the mother of invention. With a load of children, little money and long Canadian winters to get through, she had to get creative or go mad. Thankfully she got creative and consequently has done the donkey work for the rest of us. Those of you who are involved in Mother and Toddler groups and in Preschool activities will be familiar with much of what is contained here, but to have it collected in one volume will be a godsend.

There are thousands of books out there showing us how to be better parents, how to cope better, how to stimulate and entertain our children better, how to make them better human beings (at five years of age!). Quite frankly most of the ones I've read have left me with a sense of inadequacy; mostly because I needed to read them in the first place, but worst of all, inadequate because after reading them I was even more convinced that I'd never get the hang of parenting. Oh and by the way, why do so many of them have to be so smug?

Trish Kuffner's books are smug free zones, they do exactly what they say on the cover: HUNDREDS OF CREATIVE GAMES AND ACTIVITIES TO KEEP YOUR TODDLER BUSY. What more do you want?

–Mark Cagney

Introduction

'Children are the anchors that hold a mother to life.'

–Sophocles

I began writing *The Toddler's Busy Book* just as my fourth child, Johanna, was entering the toddler stage. She began to walk, then run, several months short of her first birthday and she hasn't stopped since! After surviving the baby/toddler/preschooler challenge three times with Johanna's older siblings, I'd forgotten what a trial one little toddler can be, especially an extremely active one!

But what a joy it was, too, to watch her grow and develop through the various stages of toddlerhood. Before learning to crawl and walk, she was obliged to sit wherever we put her. Now, only months later, she roams the house at will. What a treat it is to watch her as she teases her siblings and mimics her parents, to see the beginnings of imaginative play as she cuddles her 'baby', to notice the emerging concern she shows for others who are crying and to observe the development of a giving spirit as she shares her biscuit with the family cat!

Toddlerhood is a precious stage in the life of both parent and child and one which can be enjoyed immensely if you are prepared to slow down a little, sit on the floor a lot and worry about picking up the toys only when your child goes to bed at night. Organise your home to be a safe and interesting place for your child to explore and discover and introduce your child to new people, places and experiences as often as you can. Be adventurous and look at life through your child's eyes as she begins to unearth some of the many wonders of this amazing world in which we live.

The Toddler's Busy Book is intended to help you enjoy your child's toddler years. It will help you entertain and stimulate your child through the toddler years with ideas which are simple and straightforward enough for even the busiest of parents or care-givers to manage. This book contains suggestions for many situations and occasions: for indoors and outdoors, for summer and winter, for quiet times and active times. I've written this book as a resource for parents at home with their toddlers, but it is well-suited for anyone who has a toddler in his or her life: mothers, fathers, grandparents, aunts, uncles, baby-sitters, day-care providers, nursery school teachers, church workers, or playgroup leaders. If you spend any time at all with a toddler, then this book is for you.

Although many of the ideas in *The Toddler's Busy Book* may continue to entertain your child long after the toddler stage, these activities are most suitable for children between the ages of one and three. Because abilities of children in that age range vary greatly, some ideas will be too advanced for a one-year-old, while others will be much too simple for a three-year-old. Use your judgment in choosing activities that best meet the capabilities and interests of your child. If a new activity doesn't go quite as well as you expected, don't write it off altogether; try it again in a week, a month, or a year, or vary the activity in a way that will make it more meaningful and interesting for your child.

As my oldest child, my very first baby, approaches adolescence, it is a special joy to experience the toddler years again. Having several children halfway to adulthood has given me an appreciation of the brevity of the very early years of childhood–an appreciation I didn't have ten years ago when my oldest was a toddler. Although back then it seemed as though my babies would never grow up, most of them have–and yours will, too. Nappies will one day be a thing of the past, as will bottles, soothers, a bath full of toys, afternoon naps, sticky fingers, wet kisses and so many other earmarks of toddlerhood.

Each stage of childhood brings with it its own set of challenges as well as its own special rewards. Some days will bring you more joy than you ever thought possible, while on other days you'll feel grateful if you (or your children) make it through the day in one piece. This pattern doesn't change, no matter how old your children are! My hope is that you will love your child unconditionally, remember your sense of humour and relish the toddler years, because like the fingerprints on the wall, they will be gone before you know it.

Trish Kuffner

P.S. A note on the use of 'his' and 'her': In recognition of the fact that children do indeed come in both sexes and in an effort to represent each, the use of male and female pronouns will alternate with each chapter.

CHAPTER 1
Help! I Have a Toddler!

'A toddler, according to the dictionary, is one who toddles, which means "to walk with short tottering steps". Regardless of what the experts or the outsiders say, those tiny steps will plunge you into one of the most exasperating periods of your adult life.'

–Jain Sherrard

Toddlers may be described in many ways. Some call them terrible (as in 'terrible twos'); others call them 'terrific' (although I suspect those people do not currently have toddlers in their lives). Most toddlers fall somewhere in between. They are wonderful little people some days and trials on other days.

Toddlers are at an interesting stage of development. They can get around on their own, but they need constant supervision. They understand most of what they hear but are usually unable to communicate their wants and needs effectively. They want to do everything for themselves, but their skills and abilities are limited. They want to try everything and most of what they do is motivated by an interest in cause and effect. ('Let's see what happens when ...')

Toddlers also have an abundance of energy. As they enter the toddler stage, some will still be taking two naps per day, but by the end of toddlerhood, many will not be napping at all. This means that a parent or care giver must occupy the toddler for many hours each day, often without a break. This can be a challenge for most adults, whether they are encountering life with a toddler for the first time or experiencing toddlerhood for the second, third, or fourth time.

In addition to their abundant energy and desire to learn about the world around them, toddlers also have specific needs and characteristics unique to their stage of development. They are not walking babies or watered-down preschoolers. Expecting them to stay involved in activities that are not sufficiently stimulating or are too advanced for their abilities will lead to frustration for the child and the parent or care giver.

What, then, do toddlers need? What activities can a parent or care giver easily provide that will keep a toddler happy, occupied and stimulated? Parenting an infant is one thing, but coping with the specific needs of a toddler is something many of us find extremely challenging. Parents at home all day – every day – with toddlers often entertain the thought that professionals (early childhood educators or trained and experienced day care workers) could do a better job of occupying and stimulating their children.

Would your child be happier, better occupied and more stimulated if he were cared for by professionals? In certain extreme situations, the answer may be yes, but most parents lack only experience and confidence. Whether they know it or not, parents usually have what it takes to keep their toddlers happy and stimulated. Keep in mind that most of the activities in nursery and day-care centres imitate what can naturally occur in the home on a day-to-day basis: talking, singing, reading, exploring, having a snack, playing outdoors, playing with friends or siblings, napping and so on. Some may feel that the group setting of a nursery school or day care will benefit their child, but toddlers do not learn well, if at all, in group situations. Cynthia Catlin, in her book *Toddlers Together: The Complete Planning Guide for a Toddler Curriculum* (Gryphon House, 1994), says, 'Toddlers learn best through their independent explorations

15

and interactions with their care-givers, who can promote their learning by initiating activities based on the children's play behaviours and interest.'

This means parents and care-givers are instinctively doing things that stimulate their children to learn. Talking on a toy telephone, asking 'Where are your ears?' as you change your toddler, playing hide-and-seek or peek-a-boo, letting him bang about with pots and pans in the kitchen–these are activities you've done countless times without thinking you're providing a rich learning environment. You are. Running, sliding, swinging and playing outside are activities which encourage physical development. Playing with playdough, paints and crayons develops fine motor skills and promotes creativity. Washing hands before meals teaches health. 'Hot! Don't touch!' teaches safety and a short playtime with friends helps your child learn social skills.

Simply put, toddlers need a stimulating environment and a variety of experiences to help them develop. Activities which emphasise the senses and physical activity will be the most successful. A consistent daily schedule will help your child know what to expect and help him become more independent. He will enjoy repetition of the familiar in songs, books, arts and crafts and simple games and he will also be interested in anything new. Try to make a short walk or some outdoor play a part of every day. Be sure to allow your child plenty of free time with interesting things to discover and explore. We all learn best when our interest motivates us to find out about something and toddlers are no exception.

Don't rely exclusively on books like this to provide fun ideas for your toddler. Many ideas that work for others will not work for your child, or they may not work right now. Watch your child, note what interests him and go from there. Develop your own file or notebook of activities that interest your child. Some may be variations of the same activity, while others will be entirely new. Children under the age of three master skills through repetition. If something works for you, do it over and over and over again. If your child shows no interest in an activity, stop for a time and try it again in a week, month, or year.

ORGANISING FOR A TODDLER

In many cases, toddlers know how to create their own fun when given the proper materials. Although they require constant supervision, there are things you can do and materials you can provide that will encourage creative and independent play. The first step is to make sure your home is properly toddler-proofed for safety. Many small items interesting to toddlers, such as coins and beads, pose an extreme choking hazard. Make sure such items are well out of reach – an especially difficult task if you have older children in the house, too.

The following suggestions will help you better organise your home to meet your toddler's changing needs. If you have read *The Preschooler's Busy Book*, you may recognise some of these ideas (modified for toddlers, of course).

Keep a Baker's Box in the kitchen

Performing kitchen tasks can be extremely difficult when combined with keeping an eye on an energetic toddler. At times, a one-year-old may be happy just to sit in his highchair or at his own little table with a few toys or snacks to keep him occupied while you work. At other times, he will want to be right there with you, underfoot and into everything. Kitchen cupboards and drawers are full of interesting things that may prove irresistible to your child.

Why not provide your child with his very own Baker's Box? Put together a collection of unbreakable kitchen tools in a plastic crate or small storage box. Store it in a spare cupboard that is low enough for your child to reach. He can use his tools for play or for helping you do some 'real' cooking or baking. Some suggestions for a Baker's Box are:

cake tin	large metal or	pie plate
cake rack	plastic bowl	plastic measuring cups
biscuit cutters	measuring spoons	rubber spatula
baking tray	fairy cake tray	wooden spoon

Have a Busy Box handy

Since much of our time at home is spent in the kitchen, a spare kitchen cupboard low enough for your child to reach is an ideal spot for his very own Busy Box – a small storage box or plastic crate containing things he can do on his own at any time. An older toddler or preschooler will appreciate many craft supplies in his Busy Box: crayons, markers, colouring books, paper, tape, stickers, scissors, glue, ink pad and stamps, playdough and so on. But filling a Busy Box for a younger toddler is more of a challenge. Most of us don't want our one-year-olds into tape and markers without close supervision.

Items for a toddler's Busy Box must be safe enough for him to play with relatively unsupervised and they should be things that will not make a mess (at least not much of a mess). Watch what types of things interest your toddler and include those in his Busy Box. For example, if he loves playing with plastic bottles and lids, put some in the box (be sure the lids are big enough to pass the choke test). Most toddlers love to build, so add an assortment of stackable things. Items that work well are empty cereal boxes, thread spools, covered yogurt containers and individually wrapped rolls of toilet paper.

Many ideas in this book are suitable for your toddler's Busy Box. In Chapter 2, for example, you will find Sticky Figures, Texture Touch, Surprise Tins, Shaker Bottle, Who Do You See?, Postbox, Wave Bottle, Bubble Bottle, Peg Drop, Supermarket, What's in the Jar?, Fun with Tissues and Squishy Bag.

While most children have favourite things they like to play with, something new to discover and explore will hold their attention and keep them occupied. If you vary the contents of the Busy Box from day to day, your toddler will always find something fresh and exciting to keep him busy and happy.

Set up a Tickle Trunk

A Tickle Trunk full of dressing up clothes and props will not only foster your child's imaginative play but will keep him occupied with all the wonders it contains. Fill a trunk, toy box, large plastic container, or cardboard box with adult clothes, shoes, hats, scarves, gloves and costume jewellery to use for dressing up. Old suits are great, as are Hawaiian shirts, vests, baseball hats, bridesmaid dresses, nightgowns, wigs, boots, slippers and purses. Great items can be found at second-hand or thrift shops, or stock up on princess gowns and animal costumes at post-Halloween sales.

A toddler may have trouble with zippers and small buttons, so consider replacing them with Velcro or enlarging the buttonholes and replacing small buttons with large ones that are easy for little fingers to grasp.

Investing in a Tickle Trunk full of dressing up clothes may well be one of the best toys you can assemble for your toddler. Not only will it help keep him busy and happy during his early years, but chances are it will become an invaluable part of his play for many years to come.

Make up a Rainy Day Box

Although all days with babies, toddlers and preschoolers can seem long, rainy days seem to have extra hours to fill. When the weather is bad or when your child is sick, a Rainy Day Box full of surprises can help break the monotony. Good things to put in your Rainy Day Box are:

- Fresh, new art supplies (a new pad, markers, paintbox, stickers, or playdough).
- A new toy (or one that hasn't been played with in a while).
- A new book, music tape, DVD or video.
- Special dressing up items.
- Biscuit cutters and a new or favourite biscuit recipe.
- Supplies and directions for a new game or craft (pre-assemble all supplies and store them in a Ziploc bag in the Rainy Day Box until ready to use).

Don't overuse your Rainy Day Box. It will be regarded with interest and awe only if its appearance is somewhat extraordinary. Store your Rainy Day Box in a safe place and bring it out only when the day seems unusually long.

Make a Job Jar for your child

Whether you're working fulltime or staying home with your child, whether you're a day-care provider or an occasional babysitter, there will be times when housework needs to be done with your toddler close by. Instilling a sense of responsibility toward household chores is something that can be started at this tender age. (Even very young toddlers like to feel they're helping.)

You can make a Job Jar out of an empty jar or small box. Cut strips of paper and print a small job that needs to be done on each one. Very young toddlers will enjoy wiping the floor or refrigerator with a damp cloth or sponge, stacking towels in a cupboard, or picking up toys and placing them in a basket or container. You will know the jobs your child is capable of doing with minimum supervision and assistance.

Rotate your child's toys

In the first few years of life, most children receive many wonderful toys as gifts for birthdays, holidays, or other occasions. While parents appreciate the good intentions of the givers, most children have more toys than they can possibly play with. Also, even the most creative toys will fail to hold your child's interest if they're always around. When rotated every four to six weeks, toys will seem new to him and will be interesting and exciting all over again.

Separate your child's toys into piles. (If your child has a favourite toy, keep it out all the time.) Keep one pile in your child's play area and pack the others away in boxes, marking dates for when they are to be brought out. If you have friends with children the same age, why not try a toy exchange?

Keep a list of what's been exchanged and be sure to agree on the terms beforehand (how long, who's responsible for breakage and so on).

Make a Crazy Can

Someone once referred to the dinner hour as 'arsenic hour'. Once you've had a toddler or two hanging around at that time, you'll know why! This is usually the time when you are at your busiest and toddlers are at their crankiest. In the midst of the chaos, you yearn for a distraction to keep them busy. It's not a great time to brainstorm for creative activities, so plan ahead with a Crazy Can full of ideas for your toddler.

Make a list of on-the-spot activities that require no special materials, no time consuming preparation or cleaning up and no serious adult participation or supervision. Write these ideas down on index cards or small pieces of paper and put them in an empty tin. If you like, cover the tin with cheerful contact paper, or cover it with plain paper and have your child decorate it with paints, markers, or crayons. When things start to get crazy (or when there's just nothing to do), choose a card from the can for an instant remedy. Appendix B offers a list of activities appropriate for a toddler Crazy Can.

Take along a Busy Bag

A Busy Bag will help you be prepared for those times when you have to wait at the doctor's office, hairdresser's, or restaurant. Turn a drawstring bag or backpack into a take-along Busy Bag that can be filled with special goodies to keep your child amused. Borrow the portable items from your Busy Box, or take along items such as:

- Dolls and their associated clothing, blankets, bottles and accessories.
- An edible necklace (like cereal or crackers with holes in the middle strung on a piece of shoestring licorice).
- A favourite toy, stuffed animal, or blanket.
- Magnets and a small metal cake tin.
- Matchbox cars.
- Simple wooden puzzles.
- Special snacks.
- Stickers and a sticker book or plain notebook.

Use your imagination when filling the Busy Bag. You can assemble it by yourself so the contents will be a surprise for your child, or you can have your child help you fill the bag before you go. Chapter 6 contains many ideas that will help keep your toddler happy and busy when you're out and about.

Look for new activities and experiences

While children need free time for creative play and unstructured time in which to explore the world around them, they also rely on you to introduce them to new projects, activities and adventures. This is sometimes hard to do on the spur of the moment, so planning ahead is a good idea. Try to schedule one or two fun, challenging, creative activities each day (not necessarily major projects – sometimes a five-minute game will do). Decide on the activities ahead of time and assemble all the necessary supplies in advance.

PLANNING YOUR ACTIVITIES

As I mentioned in *The Preschooler's Busy Book*, failing to plan is planning to fail. That applies to the big stuff (like saving for your child's education) as well as the little stuff (like doing a new art project or playing a game with your child). Preschools and day care centres plan their curricula carefully to ensure that children have a wide variety of experiences each day. Parents at home can be somewhat less structured, but the importance of planning new and creative activities should not be overlooked. Children's activity books and resources abound and can be easily purchased or borrowed from the local library. However, the ideas in these books are only valuable if you use them. If you don't do a little planning, chances are you won't use them. Here are some helpful guidelines for planning your activities:

1. Read this book from cover to cover and create a weekly planner with activities you'd like to try each day. (Use a copy of the Weekly Activity Planner on page 31.) Include a few alternative activities for bad weather days or for when your planned activities just won't work.

2. Use your weekly activity plan to make a list of supplies you'll need and assemble or purchase them beforehand.

3. Make a list of what you need to prepare before your child becomes involved in the activity. Mix paint, assemble supplies and so on.

4. Plan special activities for your babysitter and have all the necessary materials handy. This will let your sitter know that watching TV all day is not an option.

5. Make a list of ideas that would be fun to do anytime you can fit them into your schedule. Have this list ready when you have some unexpected free time.

STOCKING YOUR CRAFT CUPBOARD

Most of the activities in this book require some basic supplies. Whether you use an actual cupboard or just a box in the basement, the following are some of the items you'll need to stock your craft cupboard.

Things to save:

aluminium pie plates (various sizes)

balls (golf, ping-pong, tennis)

bottle tops

boxes

bubble wrap

buttons

candles

cardboard

catalogues

cereal and pasta (dry)

cereal boxes

chopsticks

clean, empty food tins

coffee filters

coins

confetti containers with handles

corks

cotton balls

cotton swabs

cotton wool

dried beans

dried pasta (different shapes and sizes)

dried-up markers

egg cartons

eggshells

envelopes

fabric scraps

feathers

felt

film canisters

greeting cards (used)

jars and lids (empty)

junk mail

large, light objects to lift and carry

lids of all kinds

lolly sticks

magazines

metal biscuit tins

milk cartons (all sizes)

newspapers

old calendars

old clothes and costume jewellery for dressing up

old magazines

old mittens, socks and gloves for puppets

old sheets

old telephone books

old toothbrushes

paint sample swatches

paper bags (all sizes)

paper clips

paper fairy cake liners

paper plates/cups/bowls

paper scraps

paper towel/toilet paper tubes

photographs of friends and family

pine cones

plastic bowls, lids and bottles

plastic drinks bottles (empty)

plastic milk jugs

plastic yogurt and margarine containers

popcorn

ribbon scraps

rice (uncooked)

rocks

roll-on deodorant bottles (empty)

rubber bands

salt shakers or spice containers (empty)

sandpaper

scarves (chiffon type)

shells (large)

shoeboxes with lids

shoelaces

spray bottle

squeeze bottles (the kind ketchup comes in)

stamps

stickers of all kinds

string

Styrofoam trays

swizzle sticks

thread

thread spools

tin foil

tins with lids

tissue paper scraps

toothpicks

wood scraps

wool scraps

wrapping paper

Things to buy:

art smock (or use an old shirt)

balloons

beads (large for toddlers)

bells

chalk

child-safe scissors

clear acrylic spray

contact paper (clear and coloured)

clothes pegs (craft and springtype)

coloured cellophane

coloured tape

craft magnets

crayons

crèpe paper

elastic

fabric paint

food colouring

glitter glue

gun glue or glue sticks

googly eyes

hole punch

index cards

liquid starch

magnet strips

masking tape

newsprint rolls

paper card in various colours

paper clips

paper doilies

paper fasteners

pencil crayons

pencil sharpener

pencils

pens

pipe cleaners

plain writing pads

plastic Easter eggs

plastic tubing

pompoms

poster paints and brushes

rubber cement

ruler

sellotape

sponges

stapler stickers

straws

tissue paper

washable markers

wooden spoons

Ziploc freezer bags

WHAT ABOUT TELEVISION?

The influence of television on children has been much debated over the years. While your child may still be young enough that television is not yet an issue, be assured that it is something you will need to think about carefully in the months and years to come.

As I stated in *The Preschooler's Busy Book*, the crux of the children-and-television issue is not so much what children watch, because we can control that. I am more concerned about how parents use television and what children do not do when they watch television. It's easy to use television as a babysitter, but TV can be habit-forming to both parent and child. The few short years of early childhood are better spent playing, reading, walking, talking, painting and making things – in other words, doing things together.

However, whether we like it or not, television is here to stay. It's up to parents to use it in a way that will be beneficial to their child's development and their parent/child relationship. How should parents do this? First, be selective in what your children watch. Good television programmes can make learning fun and can expand your child's knowledge of the world. Choose wisely. Look for programmes or videotapes/DVDs which instruct, entertain and reinforce the values and principles you wish to develop in your child.

Second, limit your child's daily viewing time. Remember, time spent watching TV is time your child does not spend on other more valuable activities such as playing games, reading (or being read to), or using his imagination in countless other ways.

Third, watch TV with your child whenever possible. Most programmes move at a very fast pace to hold the attention of their young audience. But young children often have a hard time keeping track of the content and it is almost impossible for them to stop and ponder what is being presented. By watching with your child, you can provide connections that would otherwise be missed. And by reminding your child of related events in his own life, you can help him make sense of what he sees.

Finally, set an example for your child. Show him that you would rather read a book or play a game or talk to him than watch TV. It's hard to expect your child to limit his viewing and choose programmes wisely when you do just the opposite. Remember, children learn more from our actions than our words.

A WORD OF ENCOURAGEMENT

Raising a child is a monumental task which brings countless rewards, most of which will be realised only after many years of hard work. But there are also many more immediate rewards you receive daily as a parent: the first time your baby smiles at you, his first word, his first step, his warm hugs and that irresistably cute thing he did that you can't wait to tell Grandma and Grandad about. As your child moves through the various stages of early childhood from infant to toddler to preschooler, you will also see the changes that parenting is bringing about in you. You will stretch and grow as a person, you will learn new things (many of them about yourself) and you will develop more patience than you ever thought possible.

If you are parenting a preschooler and a toddler, or a toddler and an infant, or all three (or more) at the same time, the daily challenges you face are even greater. You may not be able to get out as much as you want, or do as many fun and interesting things as you'd like one-on-one with each child, but chances are if you care enough to read a book such as this, you're already doing a great job. Treasure what you've been given, keep a positive outlook on life and do the best job you can each day. (Your kids will grow up – I promise!)

Is there only one way to raise happy, healthy, confident and capable children? Of course not. But by providing your child with daily activities that are simple and fun, by placing more importance on your child's happiness and learning than on the appearance of your home and by talking to your child on a level he understands, you are well on your way to achieving this goal. Not only will he be better prepared for preschool, nursery school and the world beyond, but in the process, you'll help to make many happy memories of childhood.

Weekly Activity Planner

Week of:

To Do	To Buy
Monday	
Tuesday	
Wednesday	
Thursday	
Friday	
Saturday	
Sunday	
Rainy Day Options	

CHAPTER 2
Rainy Day Play

A Mother's Prayer:

'Dear Lord,

So far today I've done all right. I haven't gossiped, I haven't lost my temper, I haven't been greedy, grumpy, nasty, selfish, or very indulgent. I'm very grateful for that. But in a few minutes, Lord, I'm going to get out of bed and from then on, I'm going to need a lot more help. Amen.'

Most parents of very young children will agree that a bout of rainy weather can try the patience of even the calmest, most tolerant among us. Days seem longer, kids seem crankier and somehow there never seems to be enough to do to keep our energetic little ones occupied.

The west coast of British Columbia, where we live, is often called 'the wet coast'. I've had more experience than I'd care to remember of dealing with housebound babies, toddlers and preschoolers. When my three eldest children were young, there were many rainy days when everyone was up at 5 a.m., our entire day's worth of activities was completed by about 8 a.m. and there, stretching before us, were at least eight or nine more hours to fill until Daddy came home.

On days like these that seem especially neverending, my best advice is to get out of the house, if you possibly can. Call a friend and get together for lunch or a coffee. Dress everyone in rain gear and go out for a short walk. If you live close to a fast-food restaurant with a 'play place,' take advantage of it. You don't have to spend a lot. Mid-mornings and afternoons can be quite slow and owners don't usually mind you playing for an hour or two if you buy coffee or a juice. You can even go to a shopping centre just to walk around and window-shop. We had one with a big indoor fountain close by and my little girls spent a fair bit of time throwing coins into it.

But if you can't get out, for whatever reason, be prepared with lots of fun things for your little ones to do indoors. In many instances, children will create their own fun when given the proper materials:

- Put together a collection of things for your toddler to stack: Empty cereal boxes, thread spools and small yogurt containers with lids work well.
- Give your child a variety of safe, unbreakable kitchen objects so she can make her own symphony: wooden spoons, whisks, rubber spatulas, pots and pans with lids and so on.
- Place a smooth board against a chair or couch to create a ramp to roll things down.
- Help your child create simple puppets out of a paper bag and cardboard tube.
- Don't forget to look in other chapters for more great ideas for indoor fun. Kids in the Kitchen (Chapter 3), Early Learning Fun (Chapter 8), Music and Movement (Chapter 9) and of course Arts and Crafts (Chapter 10) offer countless activities to keep your toddler entertained. While the ideas in this chapter may come in especially handy on rainy days, most are suitable for every day! Many can be easily adapted for outdoor play when the weather is fair.

Inside/Outside Voice

Children are never too young to begin learning consideration for others. Even very young children can be taught this simple rule and it's a lifesaver on rainy indoor days.

Ask your child, 'How many eyes do I have?' 'How many ears do I have?' 'How many hands do I have?' Go on to explain that we all have two voices, too. One is a great, big, loud voice; the other is a smaller, softer voice. One voice is good for outside and one voice is good for inside. Ask your child, 'Which voice would be good for inside?' and 'Which voice are we using now?'

Tape City

Before taping your floor or carpet, test the tape on a small area to make sure it can be easily removed. Leaving the tape on the floor for more than a day may also make it gummy and difficult to remove.

Masking tape
Small cars

Use masking tape on your floor or carpet to create an indoor roadway for small cars. Very young children will enjoy a simple roadway to run their cars along. Older children may enjoy adding car parks, shops and schools or accessorising with dollhouses, toy people and plastic animals.

Doll Bed

Large cardboard box
Tea towels
Old baby blanket
Small pillow

Make a bed for your child's doll out of a large cardboard box. Use tea towels for bedding. Add a small pillow and a baby blanket if you have one. Your toddler will enjoy putting her baby to bed and waking her up again.

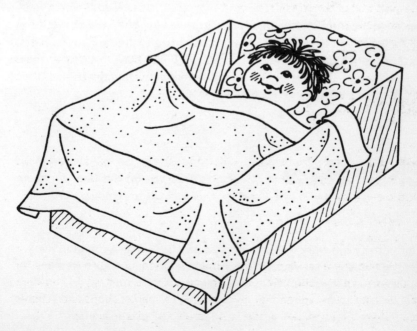

Sheet Day

Sheet Day can become an informal holiday in your house every time you strip the beds to change the sheets.

Bed sheets

Since you're stripping the beds anyway, give your child the sheets from all the beds you're changing. She can use them to create houses, tents, forts, or anything else she can dream up. When playtime is over, help your child gather up the sheets and put them in the laundry basket, then put them in the washing machine together.

Chair Maze

Chairs

This activity will work well outdoors as well as in. Place chairs in a maze around the room. Let your child crawl among them or walk over them, or use them as a train for her stuffed animals.

Sticky Figures

Flat piece of wood
Glue gun
Velcro
Small figures of animals, dinosaurs, cowboys and so on

Glue Velcro onto a flat piece of wood (use a piece that will fit on the tray of your child's highchair). Glue pieces of Velcro onto the bottom of small figures that your child likes to play with. She may amuse herself for quite a while sticking and unsticking these figures on the piece of wood. This technique could also help older children avoid frustration when scenes they are trying to set up keep falling over.

Texture Touch

Materials of varying textures: sandpaper, old carpeting, fabric, cotton balls, fun fur and so on

Metal lids

Glue

Magnets

Cut the various materials you have gathered into a round shape that will fit the lids. Glue the material onto the lid. Younger toddlers will enjoy simply feeling the textures. Magnets glued to the back of the juice lids will allow your child to play with them on the refrigerator or on a baking tray placed on the tray of her highchair. For older children, make two sets and have them sort the lids by matching the materials or sorting by texture (smoothest to roughest, softest to hardest and so on).

Sticky Feet

Clear contact paper

Tape

Cut a piece of clear contact paper at least 2 feet long. Remove the backing and tape the contact paper, sticky side up, to the floor or carpeting. Toddlers will have fun running, jumping, dancing, or just standing on the paper. Not only will their feet stick to the paper, but lifting them also makes a wonderful sound.

Surprise Tins

Stack up a few of these in the cupboards that your child explores. She will enjoy discovering what's inside.

Round metal biscuit tins with lids (or small shoeboxes with lids)

Variety of objects: plastic magnetic letters, baby-food jar lids, plastic milk-bottle caps, small blocks and so on

Fill several round, metal biscuit tins with different objects. Fill one tin with plastic milkbottle caps, another with metal baby-food jar lids, a third with small wooden blocks and so on. Stack the tins in a cupboard your child can explore. She will enjoy taking them out, shaking them, taking the lids off (maybe with your help) and discovering what's inside. You can also store things such as Texture Touch (page 38) or Picture Sort (page 164) in tins or boxes like this.

Bottles and Lids

Collection of bottles and lids of varying sizes

Save small plastic bottles with screw-type lids. Your toddler will have lots of fun matching lids to bottles, putting the lids on, taking the lids off and starting all over again. A bottle collection is also great fun for the bath, or for water play outdoors.

Shaker Bottle

Clean, empty plastic drink bottle with cap
Coloured rice or pasta
Glue gun or quick-bonding glue

Make sure the plastic drink bottle you are using is clean and dry. Place coloured rice or pasta (see Appendix A for instructions on how to dye pasta and rice) into the bottle and glue the cap on. Little ones will love to see what's happening inside as they shake and rattle their bottle.

Ice Cube Bags

Ice cube tray
Water
Red, yellow and blue food colouring
3 Ziploc bags

Mix water and food colouring (enough for two ice cubes of each colour) and pour into an ice cube tray. When frozen, place a red and a yellow ice cube into one Ziploc bag, a red and a blue ice cube into the second Ziploc bag and a yellow and a blue ice cube into the third Ziploc bag. Younger children will enjoy moving the ice cubes around in the bags, while older children will enjoy watching what happens when the two colours melt together.

Highchair Fun

Be sure to use string that is not long enough to pose a choking hazard and never leave your child unattended in her highchair.

Short lengths of string
Small toys

Tie one end of short lengths of string to a few of your child's toys. Tie or tape the other ends to the tray of her highchair. She will enjoy throwing the toys off the highchair tray, then pulling the strings to get them back again.

Who Do You See?

Small plastic mirror
Box with lid
Glue
Colourful contact paper, paper card, or wrapping paper (optional)

Glue a small mirror inside a box. Decorate the outside of the box and lid with colourful contact paper, paper card, or giftwrap. Place the lid on top of the box. When your child opens the box, she will see someone special! If you don't have a small plastic mirror and don't want your child playing with something breakable, try gluing photographs or other pictures to the inside of the box. Use photos of your child, her friends and her family or pictures of people, animals, or other objects cut from magazines or greeting cards.

Postbox

Shoebox with lid
Scissors
Unopened junk mail

Cut a large slit in the lid of a shoebox. If you like, cover the box and lid (separately) with coloured paper, or decorate with paints, markers and stickers. Place the lid on the box and show your toddler how to 'post' letters. If you don't mind her doing so, she may enjoy ripping open the letters as much as posting them. Store the post inside the box when play is over.

Fun with Tape

Simple as it may seem, a small piece of tape can provide young children with a lot of enjoyment. Collect a few different kinds of colourful plastic tape, masking tape, double-sided tape and so on. Your toddler will sometimes enjoy using tape in place of glue when making a collage.

Pieces of tape

Give your young child one or two pieces of tape to play with. She may try sticking them together, to herself, to you, or to other objects around the house. Be sure to watch her if you're worried about the tape sticking to precious books or papers that may be in her path.

Simple Sorter

If you don't have any ping-pong or golf balls handy, try using round plastic milk jug lids instead.

Ping-pong or golf balls
Plastic container with lid

Cut a hole big enough for a ping-pong or golf ball to fit through in the lid of the plastic container. Place the lid on the container and let your toddler have fun poking the balls through the hole. She will quickly learn how to remove the lid to retrieve the balls, but will need your help to replace the lid on the container so she can start over again.

Threading

Shoelace or thin plastic tubing

Items for threading: empty thread spools, large beads, hair curlers, tubular pasta, paper towel tubes cut into 1-inch rings

Collect a variety of round objects such as empty spools, large beads, plastic hair curlers, large tubular pasta, or paper towel tubes cut into 1inch rings. Show your child how to thread these items onto a shoelace or length of thin plastic tubing. Tie one of the objects being threaded to the end of the lace or tubing to prevent the rest from slipping off.

Wave Bottle

Clean, empty plastic drink bottle with cap

Water

Food colouring

Glitter, sequins, or beads (optional)

Baby oil

Quick-bonding glue

Fill the clean plastic bottle with water to about one-third full. Add a few drops of food colouring and glitter, sequins, or beads (optional), then fill the rest of the bottle with baby oil. Glue the cap securely onto the bottle by applying the glue to the inside of the bottle cap and screwing it on. Your child will enjoy gently shaking the bottle to produce beautiful waves.

Peg Tin

Craft-type clothes pegs (without springs)
Empty tin

Show your toddler how to place the clothes pegs around the rim of a tin. You can also cut a small hole in the plastic lid of the can and have her drop the clothes pegs through the hole. She'll like the sound they make as they hit the bottom. Store the clothes pegs in the covered tin when not in use.

Peg Drop

Large clean plastic milk bottle with lid
6–8 clothes pegs

Put the clothes pegs in the bottle and screw on the lid. Your toddler will enjoy shaking the bottle with the clothes pegs inside. Show her how to remove the lid (or do it for her if she can't quite do it on her own), shake the clothes pegs out, then drop them back in again one by one. For variety, try using a couple of spoons in place of clothes pegs. They make an interesting sound when the bottle is shaken.

Bubble Bottle

Clean, large, empty plastic drink bottle with cap
Water
Poster paint
1/3 cup washing up liquid

Fill the clean plastic bottle with water to about one-third full. Add a spoon or two of poster paint and the washing up liquid. Glue the cap securely onto the bottle by applying glue to the inside of the bottle cap and screwing it on. Your child will enjoy shaking the bottle to make coloured bubbles.

For a quick and easy alternative, put small pieces of wool (about 3–6 inches long) into a clean, empty plastic bottle. Fill the bottle with water and glue the cap on. Your child will enjoy shaking the bottle to make the wool dance.

Ring Fun

Rubber rings
Wooden spoon
Playdough (See Appendix A for recipe)
Small plastic container

Fill a small plastic container with playdough and insert a wooden spoon in the middle. (If you want to keep your child's fingers out of the playdough, use a container with a lid; cut a hole in the lid big enough for the wooden spoon to go through.) Give your child a stack of rubber canning rings and show her how to place the rings over the end of the wooden spoon.

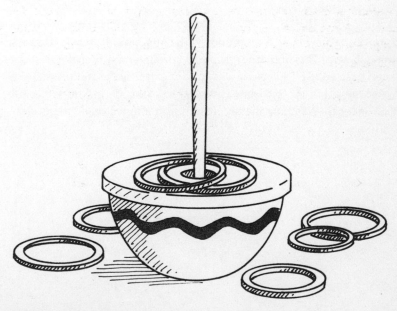

Indoor Sandbox

In *The Preschooler's Busy Book*, I suggest making an indoor sandbox by filling up a cardboard box or plastic baby bathtub with puffed wheat or rice cereal or uncooked rice. Here are some alternatives that may be purchased fairly inexpensively in bulk. They provide an interesting sensory experience for toddlers.

> *water softener salt*   *foam packing peanuts*
> *porridge oats*   *birdseed*
> *shredded paper*   *dried beans*
> *potting soil (if you're brave!)*

Children enjoy playing in the sandbox with cups, spoons, bowls, buckets, scoops, shovels, cars and other toys and containers. A funnel and scoop that can be used to fill an empty plastic soda bottle with sandbox material will also be a hit. An old sheet, shower curtain, or plastic tablecloth placed under the sandbox makes cleaning up afterwards a little easier.

Clothes Peg Poke

Empty egg carton
Clothes pegs

Turn the egg carton upside down and punch small holes (just big enough to fit the peg) in the bottom of each section. Place clothes pegs in the holes and let your toddler have fun taking them out and putting them back in again.

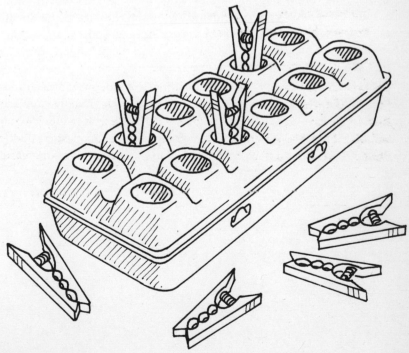

Supermarket

Toddlers have fun filling up bags and baskets with just about anything. For variety, use blocks or Lego in place of the shopping suggested here.

Paper bag with handles or small basket
Empty food boxes and containers

Save up empty food boxes and containers. Cereal boxes, small yoghurt containers and empty vitamin bottles work well. Seal the boxes with tape, then use a glue gun to permanently attach the lids to the small containers. (They may be a choking hazard.) Store all your 'shopping' in a box or laundry basket. Your child will have fun 'going shopping' with a paper bag or small basket.

Rock Play

Johanna, my toddler-in-residence while I was writing this book, loved to play with rocks. No matter where we were outside, she was sure to be found playing with rocks. Of course rocks found their way inside and we found them everywhere: with her toys, in her cot, in the bath and inside cupboards. She never seemed to tire of her little rock collection.

Rocks
Containers
Basket with handle

Take your toddler for a walk outside. Bring along a plastic bucket or basket with handles and collect rocks as you walk. Be sure to choose rocks big enough to pass the choke test (or simply discard the smaller ones when you return home).

When you get home, wash the rocks and set them out with some containers for your child to play with. She will enjoy placing them one by one in the containers, tipping them out, carrying them around with her in a basket and putting them in her pockets or purse. She may also enjoy painting them or placing them in a covered tin to make a loud shaker toy.

What's in the Jar?

Toddlers always love taking lids off small containers and jars. It's even more fun when there's an interesting toy inside!

Small clear plastic jars with lids
Small toys that will fit into each jar

Place a small, colourful toy into a clear plastic jar and close the lid. Give your toddler the jar and let her remove the lid and retrieve the toy inside. She'll probably want to do it again and again.

Where's Teddy?

Teddy bear or soft toy
Long string

Tie one end of a long string around one of your child's soft toys or her favourite teddy bear. Hide the bear under a bed or in a closet or drawer. Trail the string from the bear's hiding place around the room, over and under furniture, out the door and down the hall as far as you like. Give the end of the string to your child and say, 'Where's Teddy?' (or use the toy's name). Help her follow the string to find the bear.

Bear in the Basket

What parent hasn't come into a child's room after their nap and discovered every doll, bear, animal and blanket on the floor? Children won't need much help catching on to this game!

Stuffed animals
Large basket or container

Place a large basket or container next to your child's cot (empty laundry baskets or hampers work well). Place her in the cot along with a teddy bear or supply of stuffed animals or other soft, light toys. Show her how to drop the bear into the basket. You may want to count to her, 'One, two, three, drop the bear!'

Fun with Tissues

Most toddlers have probably tried this on their own at one time or another.

Box of tissues

Give your toddler a box of tissues and let her pull the tissues out one by one. The fun your toddler will have and the time she spends on this will justify the price of the box of tissues! If you'd rather not use real tissues, stuff a few scarves or pieces of brightly coloured tissue paper into an empty tissue box and let your child pull those out instead.

Nuts and Bolts

Large nuts and bolts

Purchase several large nuts and bolts and keep them on hand for your older child (probably three and up). She will enjoy screwing nuts on and off the bolts and you can use this as a counting activity, too.

Nesting Cans

I bought a popular set of twelve nesting cups when my first child was an infant. Ten years later, I don't think anyone (other than myself) has ever put all twelve cups back in order! Three or four cups or cans are sufficient for most toddlers.

3–4 cans that fit inside one another
Duct tape
Scissors
Contact paper or paper card

Make a set of nesting cans by saving three or four cans that fit inside one another. Make sure there are no sharp edges, then cover the rim of each can with duct tape. Cover each can with contact paper or paper card. Your child will have fun tipping out the cans, then fitting them back together. Turn the cans upside down to build a tower.

For a sorting activity, make two or three sets of nesting cans. Cover each set in a different colour or pattern of contact or paper card.

Toddler Train

Your child will enjoy filling up each carriage with her stuff and pulling the train behind her wherever she goes.

3 or more assorted boxes
String, ribbon, or wool
Plastic straws
Scissors

Use scissors or another pointed object to poke small holes in the ends of each box. Insert about 1 foot of string, ribbon, or wool into the back hole of the first box, then tie the end of the string around a short piece of plastic straw to prevent it from pulling through the hole. Insert the other end of the string through the front hole of the next box and fasten it in the same way. Use more string to continue connecting the boxes until the train is finished. Use a longer length of string for the front hole of the first box. Tie a cylindrical wooden block or small plastic vitamin bottle to the end of this string for a handle.

Pull Box

Small box without lid
Thick rope

Punch a small hole in one end of the small box (a shoebox is ideal). Insert one end of the rope through the hole and tie a knot so that the rope will not pull through the hole. Your child will have fun filling her box with blocks, rocks, small toys, or other objects and pulling it behind her around the room or outside on a walk.

Potty Pals

I've never used this idea myself, but one mother says it's the only thing that helped get her three-year-old out of nappies.

Colourful contact paper
Scissors

Cut out eyes and a smile from contact paper and stick them to the underside of each toilet seat your child will be using. (Don't forget your child's potty, if she has one.) Your child can name the potty pals and assume responsibility for 'feeding' them throughout the day. This idea can make going to the potty an exciting event rather than something to avoid.

Blanket Riding

This activity works best on smooth flooring such as hardwood, linoleum, or ceramic.

Blanket, sheet, or large towel

Sit your child in the middle of a blanket, sheet, or large towel. Grasp the edge of the blanket and gently pull her around the room.

Jungle Safari

This is a great way to get your toddlers and preschoolers to bed at night.

Stuffed animals
Torch

Just before bedtime, when pyjamas are on and teeth are brushed, hide your child's stuffed animals in odd places around the house (for very young children, you may have to hide them in rather obvious places at first). Turn off the lights and use a torch to hunt for the animals hiding in your house.

Nursing Basket

This is a great idea for the toddler who seems to need something every time you sit down to nurse or feed your new baby. This idea also works well when you need to make a few phone calls without interruptions.

Small basket, box, drawstring bag, or plastic storage container

Snacks, special toys, books and so on

Put together a nursing basket for your toddler by assembling a collection of special snacks, toys, books, or other treats that can be brought out only when you nurse the baby. When you're finished nursing or feeding your baby, put the basket away until the next time.

Hedgehog Playdough

Playdough (See Appendix A for recipes)

Wooden lolly sticks or plastic drinking straws

Give your child a lump of playdough and a bunch of wooden lolly sticks or plastic drinking straws. Show her how to poke the sticks or straws into the playdough to make a hedgehog.

Monkey, Monkey!

Too often parents focus on the bad things children do, while letting the good slip by without comment. This is a simple way to reinforce and reward cooperation and kindness.

Plastic linking monkeys

Hang a plastic monkey on the wall in a place where you can add more monkeys to make a chain. When you catch your child being especially kind and cooperative (that is, playing quietly with siblings, helping out without being asked, picking up toys without being reminded and so on), reward her with a monkey to add to the chain. When the last monkey is hung, treat the whole family to an ice-cream sundae, DVD, or special afternoon of games.

People Puppets

Photos of family members
Glue or tape
Clear contact paper
Lolly sticks

Use glue or tape to attach a lolly stick to the back of a photograph. Cover with clear contact paper for an instant puppet.

Napkin Bug

Even much older children will have fun with this one.

Paper towel
Medium-size orange, grapefruit, or plastic ball
Pen or marker

Place the orange, grapefruit, or plastic ball on a flat surface and put one piece of paper towel over it so that the fruit is roughly centred under the towel. Cup your hand over the paper towel so that it moulds around the fruit (this is the body of the bug). Using your other hand, twist each corner of the paper towel until you have twisted right up to the body (these are the legs). Use a pen or marker to draw a face on the bug, then roll the fruit to make the bug run (the rather jerky roll of the fruit gives the bug a funny little run). If you like, make a couple of bugs and race them against each other.

i Think i Can

Ask your child if she thinks she can do something that may seem hard at first, then play the 'I Think I Can' game. Ask your child to try different things like 'Can you hop on one foot?' or 'Can you touch your toes?' Demonstrate for her, then say 'I think I can, I think I can' as you hop or bend together. Try this game when you're encouraging your child to pick up her toys. ('Do you think you can put away all your cars before I pick up these puzzles?')

Interrupt Rule

I wish I had come across this idea when my children were younger. Although they've always been polite interrupters, even 'Excuse me, Mummy' repeated twenty times can be annoying. Worse still is the adult who breaks off mid-sentence to turn full attention to the interrupting child.

When you're talking on the phone or in person with someone, teach your child how to interrupt politely. Show her how to place her hand on your arm, shoulder, or leg. This will be her signal that she needs your attention. Place your hand over hers as your signal that you understand and will acknowledge her as soon as politely possible. Very young children should not be made to wait more than 10 or 15 seconds, but this time can and should grow longer as your child becomes used to this rule.

Mini Mask

Paper
Scissors
Pencil, markers, or crayons
50-cent coin

Cut a small (4- to 6-inch) square of paper. Place the coin in the middle of the square and trace around it. Draw eyes above the circle and a mouth below it. Be creative in adding eyelashes, eyebrows, or a funny moustache. Cut out the eyes and nose and put the mask on your child's face by placing the centre hole over her nose.

Early Morning Fun

If your toddler is an early riser, you may find this idea will give you a few extra minutes of precious sleep.

Basket or small plastic crate
2–3 quiet toys, games, or activities

Before you go to bed at night, put two or three quiet toys, games, or activities in a basket or small plastic crate. Be sure that the items you choose are completely safe for your child to play with unsupervised. Place the basket or crate in your toddler's cot or beside her bed. The toys or activities may keep her occupied long enough for you to make the coffee, have a shower, or just enjoy a little extra sleep!

Cartons of Fun

This idea is recommended for older two- and three-year-olds, as younger children are not likely to get any more creative than tipping the contents on the floor.

Empty milk cartons or other containers
Miscellaneous craft items

Fill clean empty milk cartons with an assortment of craft items: scraps of fabric, ribbon, wrapping paper, bows, stickers, glue, safety scissors and so on. Bring out the carton for a fun and creative playtime.

Cereal Box Puzzle

A colourful cereal box can make an inexpensive jigsaw puzzle tailored to your child's age and ability.

Empty cereal box
Scissors

Cut out the front panel of an empty cereal box. Cut into interlocking shapes, making the size of the pieces and the difficulty of the puzzle appropriate for the child who will be putting the puzzle together.

Easy Bird Feeder

Feeding the birds is fun, but once you start, it's important to keep it up for the whole season. Birds will come to rely on the food you provide and may have difficulty finding another food source if you suddenly stop.

Round / circular oat cereal or circular pretzels
Heavy string, wool, or a shoelace

String round oat cereal bits onto heavy string, wool, or a shoelace. Tie the ends together and hang in a tree to feed the birds.

Squishy Bag

3 cups water
4 tablespoons cornflour
Food colouring
Ziploc bag

Boil the water. In a separate bowl, add cold water to the cornflour to make a paste. Slowly add the cornflour mixture to the boiled water. Cook and stir until thick. Add food colouring and allow to cool. Pour into a Ziploc bag and seal. Children can squish the bag without opening it.

Magic Mud

Kids of all ages love this one. Magic Mud feels like a solid, but it just drips through your fingers.

1 box cornflour
Water
Food colouring

Put the cornflour in a bowl. Add just enough water to be able to stir the mixture, then add food colouring. Your child may want to use her fingers to play with this, but it's great for running cars through, too.

Flying Fish

Your child will enjoy tossing these fish into the air and watching them gently flutter down.

Page from an old magazine
Pencil
Ruler
Scissors

Using the ruler, pencil and scissors, mark and cut a strip of the magazine page that is as long as the page and 1 inch wide. Mark a line on each end of the strip that is 1 inch from the end. Cut a slit halfway into the strip at each point. (At one end of the strip cut from the top halfway down to the middle and at the other end cut from the bottom halfway up to the middle.) Bend the strip into a loop and push the slits together so that the loop closes. Toss the fish into the air to see it fly.

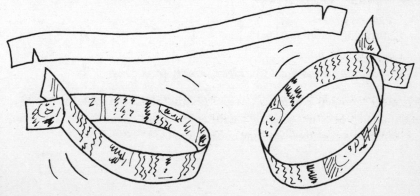

No-Cook Squishy Bag

Try the following no-cook alternatives to the Squishy Bag. Make sure the bag is well-sealed before letting your child squish it. You can vary the sensory experience by warming or chilling the contents before giving the bag to your toddler. You could also use two bags at a time – one warm and one cold.

Hair gel and a few drops of food colouring
Ketchup and mustard
Shaving cream with or without food colouring
Toothpaste
Hand lotion
Thick finger-paint

People Blocks

Pictures of family members
Clear contact paper
Rectangular wood blocks or clean, empty food cans

Use clear contact paper to attach photographs of your family to rectangular blocks of wood or clean, empty food cans. Your child will love building structures with her people blocks.

Painting Bag

Although this idea uses paint, I think it's too neat and clean to include with the other painting activities. It's quick and fun for any time – not just when you've got the time and energy for a painting project.

3 tablespoons powdered poster paint
¼ cup liquid starch (optional)
Ziploc bag
Paper card

Mix the powdered poster paint with liquid starch. Pour it into the bag and smooth out the bubbles. If you don't have liquid laundry starch, just use finger-paint. Make sure the bag is well-sealed, then show your child how to press the bag to make designs. Place a piece of paper card under the bag (use a different colour than the paint) and notice how it seems to change the colour of the paint.

Toddler Pouch

Toddlers love to collect things in their pockets. Your child will enjoy wearing this little pouch and using it to store all her interesting discoveries.

> *2 paper plates*
> *Scissors*
> *Stapler*
> *Hole punch*
> *Wool or ribbon*

Cut one paper plate in half. Staple one half to the second paper plate to form a pouch. Punch two holes in the top of the full paper plate, then tie a short length of wool or ribbon from one hole to the next to form a handle. (Because of the danger of strangulation, please make sure that the wool or ribbon is not long enough to go over your child's head.) Decorate it with crayons, markers, or stickers. Hang the pouch from your child's belt or let her carry it around with her.

Pipe Play

10 to 20-foot length of 1-inch PVC pipe
PVC joints

Cut a 10- to 20-foot length of 1 inch PVC pipe into various lengths ranging from 4 to 10 inches. Add various PVC joints to serve as connectors. (These come straight or in a T, L or + shape.) Your child should have years of fun building structures with these pipes and connectors.

In fine weather, your child will enjoy building things outside. Add a garden hose so she can run water through her pipes.

Tubes and Balls

Small balls such as golf balls, ping-pong balls, or tennis balls
Cardboard tubes from empty paper towel rolls or large gift wrap rolls
Scissors
Box or basket

Collect a variety of small balls that are big enough to avoid a choking hazard. Cut various widths of cardboard tubes into different lengths. Put the balls and tubes in a box or basket and let your child have fun dropping the balls through the tubes.

Tube Fun

A short length of flexible transparent tubing from the hardware store can be used in several ways to provide some simple fun for your toddler.

3-foot length of flexible transparent tubing, about 1 inch in diameter
Marbles
Cork
Glue gun
Vegetable oil

Glue a cork securely in one end of the tube. Put several marbles inside the tube and glue a cork in the other end. Your child will have fun seeing the marbles roll as she lifts the tube by one end or in the middle.

For an alternative, use a shorter length of tubing and fill with vegetable oil before adding the marbles. (Be sure the corks fit very tightly for this one!)

Tube Ball

Large cardboard poster tube or wrapping paper tube
Tennis ball
String
Empty basket or box

Tie a large cardboard tube to a stair rail, making the end of the tube even with the end of the railing. Place a basket or box at the end of the tube. Your toddler will enjoy placing the ball in one end and watching it shoot out the other end into the basket. This will keep your little one busy for a long time, especially if she has to climb down the steps to retrieve the ball and back up to play again.

If you don't want her climbing the steps on her own, give her a small stool to step on to reach the top end of the tube, or avoid stools and steps altogether by placing one end of the tube on a couch and the other end on the floor.

Net Ball

This makes a big, light ball that's safe and easy for even the youngest child to use indoors or out.

Onion-bag netting
Cotton batting or cotton balls
Twist tie or elastic band

Stuff the onion-bag netting with as much cotton as possible. Knot the top of the bag with a twist tie or elastic band.

Fun with Balls

Fairy cake tray
Tennis, golf, or ping-pong balls
Small basket or plastic container with handle (optional)

Give your toddler several tennis, golf, or ping-pong balls (or an assortment of all three) and an empty muffin pan. She will have fun putting the balls in each compartment, dumping them out, gathering them up and starting all over again. If you like, provide her with a small basket or plastic container into which she can put the balls as she picks them up.

Toddler Blocks

Even number of empty milk cartons (any size will do)
Tape
Colourful contact paper, fabric, paper card
or wrapping paper

Choose two milk cartons the same size. Measure the base of one carton and mark a cutting line that same distance up the side of the carton. Cut along the line. Cut the other carton in the same way. You should now have two open-ended cubes. Push one cube open-end-down into the other cube. Tape around the cut edges.

The cubes you make can be covered in any way you like. Use colourful contact paper, paper card, fabric, or wrapping paper. You can also glue on photos of your child, her friends and family, or pictures from magazines. If using paper card, wrapping paper, photos, or pictures, cover with clear contact paper to make the block more durable.

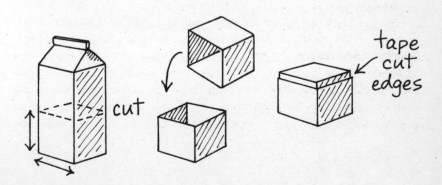

cut

tape
cut
edges

Balls, Balls, Balls

Children get so much enjoyment from balls. Instead of using a 'real' ball, try using rolled-up socks, crumpled-up newsprint taped into a ball, or make a Net Ball (see page 74). These ideas can be easily adapted for either indoor or outdoor play.

Soft ball
Empty box or laundry basket
Slide or board

1. Sit opposite your child with your legs apart and take turns rolling the ball back and forth to each other.
2. Turn the box or basket on its side and show your child how to roll the ball into the target.
3. Place an empty box or laundry basket on the floor and have your child toss the ball into the basket from several feet away.
4. Place the basket on top of a dresser for a game of indoor basketball.
5. Using a slide or a board propped against a chair or the stairs, show your child how to roll the ball down it. Then try rolling the ball up the slide or board.

Sponge Blocks

Sponges make ideal blocks for toddlers. They are easy to hold, lightweight and won't hurt anybody or anything if thrown.

Large, thick sponges

Purchase a colourful variety of large, thick sponges for your toddler to use as blocks. If you like, cut some in halves, quarters, triangular shapes, or other shapes. Store them in a laundry basket or plastic storage bin. Older toddlers may enjoy sorting sponges by colour or making a pattern with them.

Stacking Fun

Individually wrapped toilet paper rolls
Small cans of tuna, tomato paste and so on

Look around your house for interesting items for your toddler to stack. If you buy toilet paper in individually wrapped rolls, your child will have great fun using them to build towers. Small cans of tuna or tomato paste also stack nicely and are easy for little hands to manage.

Paper Bag Blocks

Toddlers love to lift and carry these big, light blocks. They're rather hard to store but easy to make again another day.

Paper bags
Newspapers
Packing tape

Lay a paper bag flat on a floor or table. Fold the top over 6–8 inches and make a crease. Scrunch up newspaper one sheet at a time and fill the bag to the fold line. Fold the top over and tape the bag closed. If you like, paint or decorate the blocks before using. Make a tunnel for your child to crawl through or a tower for her to knock down or just let her carry the blocks around the house.

Balloon Fun

Balloons
String
Plastic baseball bat, plastic golf club,
Wrapping paper tube, or rolled-up newsprint

Inflate five or six balloons and tie the ends securely. Attach a length of string or ribbon to each balloon. Suspend the bunch of balloons from the ceiling so that they hang just beyond your child's reach. Let your toddler use a plastic baseball bat or golf club to bat at the bunch of balloons. If you don't have a bat or golf club, use a cardboard giftwrap tube, or make a bat by rolling up several sheets of newsprint and taping them securely. Remember to supervise carefully when young children are playing with balloons.

Hide the Beanbag

Beanbag

Have your child close her eyes while you hide a beanbag within a defined area. When she finds the beanbag, it's her turn to hide it while you close your eyes.

More Balloon Fun

1 or more helium-filled balloons
String or ribbon

Attach a length of string or ribbon to a helium-filled balloon. The string or ribbon should be just long enough so that your child can reach the string when the balloon is resting on the ceiling. Your child will have fun pulling the balloon down, letting it go and watching it rise back up to the ceiling again. Supervise carefully to avoid the danger of your child choking on a piece of broken balloon.

Beanbag Throw

Beanbag
Basket

Throw a beanbag into a basket and ask your child to bring you the beanbag. Repeat as long as this holds her attention. She may want to try throwing the beanbag into the basket herself or may just walk to the basket and drop it in.

Beanbag Crawl

Beanbag

Place a beanbag on your child's back while she's in a crawling position. Have her crawl around the room until the beanbag falls off. Two toddlers will enjoy playing this game, with one crawling and the other picking up the beanbag when it falls. Older children can play with a friend or sibling, seeing who can keep the beanbag on her back the longest.

Beanbag Races

One child can race against the clock, while two or more children can race against either the clock or each other.

Beanbag
Clock (optional)

Decide on a starting line and a finish line. Have children race with a beanbag balanced on their head or squeezed between their knees. For very young children, try balancing the beanbag in an open palm or kicking the beanbag across the finish line.

Indoor Baseball

Games such as this help your toddler develop eye-hand coordination and are suitable for indoor as well as outdoor play.

Empty wrapping paper roll
Balloon

Play baseball with an inflated balloon and an empty giftwrap roll. Take turns hitting, throwing and running bases. Due to the extreme choking hazard posed by pieces of broken balloon, remember to always supervise carefully when young children are playing with balloons.

Toddler Bowling

Empty plastic drinks bottles or unopened paper towel rolls
Large rubber ball

Line up three or four (or more) empty plastic drinks bottles or unopened paper towel rolls. Show your toddler how to roll a large rubber ball to knock them over.

Balloon Play

Remember: balloon pieces can pose an extreme choking hazard for children, so any balloon play with toddlers must be carefully supervised.

Wooden paint stirrer / wooden spoon
Large paper plate
Glue gun
Balloons

Use a glue gun to attach a large paper plate to the end of a wooden spoon or paint stirrer. Throw the balloon up in the air and ask your toddler to try to catch the balloon in the paper plate, or have fun simply batting the balloon around. Put on some lively music to add to the fun.

Mini Olympics

Paper plates and/or straws
Newspaper
Marker

Make a bull's-eye by drawing a large circle on a sheet of newspaper. Standing back a few feet, have your child try to throw a 'discus' (paper plate) so that it lands on the bull's-eye. Vary this game by using drinking straws as javelins.

Toddler Obstacle Course

An obstacle course is great fun for a group of toddlers at a birthday party, playgroup, or other group setting. You can also use it at home for your own toddler or preschooler.

Come up with fun ideas for an obstacle course for your child or group. Bear in mind the ages, abilities and number of children who will be involved, as well as the space you have available. Keep it simple to start with and change the components of the course as they are mastered. Keep in mind that a toddler will need the help of an older child or adult to make it through the obstacle course, especially the first time.

The following ideas will get you started. Four or five stations are probably enough for a very young group. (Older preschoolers should be able to manage up to ten.)

- Jump over a rope.
- Walk along a balance board or a line of tape on the floor.
- Build a tower with blocks or other stackable objects.
- Roll a ball into a target or down a slide.
- Clip clothes pegs around the rim of a tin.
- String some beads on a shoelace.
- Draw a picture or scribble on a piece of paper.
- Play a game of newspaper golf with a rolled-up newspaper and a golf ball.
- Drop objects into a simple shape sorter.
- Play a simple matching game (correctly match up two sets of objects).
- Knock down paper towel rolls or empty drinks bottles with a large ball.
- Thread rubber rings on a wooden spoon.
- Crawl among or walk over chairs placed in a maze around the room.
- Jump into and out of a hula-hoop two or more times.

Big Mouth Game

Cardboard box
Markers
Scissors
Newspaper or tissue paper for decorating
Glue
Tennis balls or rolled-up pairs of socks

Draw a happy face on the side of a closed cardboard box. Make sure to draw a big, smiling, open mouth. Cut out the mouth. Add hair to the top of the box by gluing strips of newspaper or tissue paper so they hang down the sides. Stand back a suitable distance and see how many balls can be thrown into the mouth.

Musical Animals

This is an easier and more suitable (for younger children) version of the familiar musical chairs game.

> *1 stuffed animal for each player*
> *1 chair for each player (optional)*
> *Music*

Place several chairs in a circle and put a stuffed animal on each chair, or place the animals in a circle on the floor. Toddlers walk around the circle and, when the music stops, each player picks up an animal and sits down. Players then take turns acting out that animal. If you don't have enough stuffed animals, paste pictures of various animals on sheets of paper and tape them to the chairs or place them in a circle on the floor.

If only you and your child are playing this game, try placing the stuffed animals inside a pillowcase. Then take turns removing an animal from the pillowcase and acting it out.

Unwrapping Game

Small toy
Wrapping paper
Tape

Wrap a small toy in wrapping paper. Show the wrapped toy to your toddler and ask, 'What do you think is inside?' Give the wrapped toy to your child so she can remove the paper. Then re-wrap the toy as your child watches. Let her unwrap it again and repeat the game until she tires of it.

Torch Fun

Torch

Shine a flashlight on different parts of a room: a wall, the door, the floor and so on. Each time you shine the light on an object, name it: for example, 'This is the bed.' Show your child how to turn the flashlight on and off. Let her shine it on various objects and name them. Give her directions to follow, such as 'Shine the light on the ceiling'.

CHAPTER 3
Kids in the Kitchen

'Children are natural mimics – they act like their parents in spite of every attempt to teach them good manners.'

– *Anonymous*

Several times throughout this book you will read that for toddlers, it's the process – not the product – that counts. The value of an activity comes from what they do and what they learn rather than what they produce. That's certainly worth remembering for most activities, such as art and crafts, but in the kitchen it's a rather different story. In the kitchen the product does count! Kids may have fun dumping in a whole box of salt and they may learn that salt comes quickly from the box when you turn it upside down, but unfortunately you will end up with an inedible product and a disappointed child!

A one-year-old will often be happy to sit in his highchair or at his own table with a small container of cereal or raisins to occupy him while you work. An empty egg carton to put his little snacks in will often keep him busy for a long time. But if he insists on helping, there are lots of ways to accommodate him without putting your delicious food in danger:

- Bake fairy cakes and mix frosting ahead of time and let your toddler frost the fairy cakes with a small plastic knife or lolly stick.
- When making biscuits, roll a bit of dough into a log and let your child use a plastic knife or lolly stick to cut the log into small pieces.

- Let your child pour pre-measured ingredients and stir whenever possible.
- Give your child lettuce to tear for a salad and dressing to shake in a tightly closed plastic container.

The kitchen can be a great learning environment for your toddler, but the many irresistible things to see, touch, taste and smell also make it a hazardous place for unsupervised children. Always be safety conscious. Make sure any dangerous objects are well out of reach and closely supervise any use of sharp utensils, the oven, or the microwave. Better yet, make a rule that only an adult can use those things.

The activities in this chapter suggest fun ways for toddlers to become involved in the preparation of food.

Letter Sandwiches

Alphabet cereal
Sliced wheat bread
Peanut butter, jam, or honey

Spread a few slices of bread with peanut butter, jam, or honey. Help your older toddler spell his name or a simple sentence such as 'I love you' by applying the appropriate alphabet letters to his slice of bread. Younger toddlers will probably enjoy simply sticking the letters onto the bread in no particular order.

Homemade Butter

Heavy cream
Baby-food jar or other small jar with a tight-fitting lid
Sieve or cheesecloth

Place the cream in the jar and cover it tightly with a lid. Your child can shake and shake and shake the jar until the cream forms soft lumps. Drain the lumpy cream through a sieve or cheesecloth and discard the liquid. Mash the remaining lumps in a bowl until they're smooth. Serve on muffins, bread, or crackers for a tasty snack.

Fruit Dips

Long plastic straws
Fruit cut into chunks
Yogurt (optional)

Cut a variety of fruits into chunks. These could include orange cubes, pineapple pieces, apple squares, strawberry bites, peach parts, whole grapes (or halves for very young children) and banana chunks. Show your child how to slide the pieces onto a long plastic straw. Eat them as is or dip them into yogurt for a great tasting, fun-to-eat snack.

Jelly Paints

2–3 different colours of jelly

Prepare two or three different colours of jelly ahead of time. When set, place globs of each colour on a tabletop, highchair tray, plastic or paper plate, or other smooth surface. Your child will have fun mucking about with this tasty fingerpaint and eating it will not harm him!

What is it?

Scarf for blindfolding
Various objects to touch, smell and taste

Challenge your child's senses by blindfolding him and giving him objects to identify using his sense of touch, smell and taste. Very young children (or children who object to being blindfolded) can simply close their eyes. Start with something easy such as a banana or cracker. Try non-food items as well (a feather or a favourite toy) and be prepared to take a turn at the challenge yourself.

Picture Menus

If you like to give your child a choice at mealtime, but he tends to want the same meals day after day, picture menus may be the answer.

Pictures of your child's favourite meals
Heavy paper
Glue
Magnetic clip

Plan several different meals that you know your child likes, being sure to include a variety of healthy foods (fruits or vegetables, protein foods and grains) in each one. Cut out pictures of each meal from supermarket flyers, coupons, product labels, or magazine pictures. Glue the pictures to index cards or pieces of heavy paper (one meal per page) and hang them on a magnetic clip on the refrigerator. After your child chooses a meal he'd like, move that card to a different location until all the cards have been used up, then start over. Your child still has a choice, but there will be less arguing, indecision and monotony.

Butterfly Sandwich

Bread
Cream cheese, peanut butter, or other bread spread
Bananas, raisins, pickles and vegetable slices

Create an open-faced butterfly sandwich by cutting a slice of bread diagonally, then reversing the halves to form a butterfly. Spread with cream cheese, peanut butter, or other bread spread, then decorate with pickles, banana slices, raisins, or other pieces of soft fruit. Cut carrots or peppers in thin strips for antennae.

Vegetable Teethers

Frozen mixed vegetables

Serve your teething toddlers frozen mixed vegetables straight from the freezer. Most kids like them better uncooked and they can be a quick fix for those fussy times.

Apple Smile

Red apple (unpeeled)
Peanut butter
Miniature marshmallows

Cut a crisp apple into wedges. When laid on its side, each wedge should look like a lip. Spread one side of an apple wedge with peanut butter. Add three or four miniature marshmallow 'teeth' along the edge. Spread another apple wedge with peanut butter. Place it on top of the marshmallows for a big, toothy grin.

No-Bake Banana Biscuits

Crackers
Rolling pin
Ziploc bag
Banana or other fruit

Place three crackers in a Ziploc bag and crush them with a rolling pin. Slice a banana or other fruit into small pieces. Shake a few pieces at a time into the bag to completely coat the fruit. Lay the pieces out on a plate and, if you like, provide a little fork for spearing.

Ants on a Log

This easy, no-bake treat is fun to make and healthy, too!

Celery stalks
Small plastic knife or lolly stick
Peanut butter
Raisins

Wash and cut celery stalks into 3-or 4-inch sticks. Give your child a small plastic knife or a lolly stick and show him how to spread peanut butter onto the celery. Stick raisins in the peanut butter and eat. If your child has an allergy to peanut butter, use cheese spread, cream cheese, jam, or honey.

Fruit lollies

Baby food (or puréed fruit)
Unsweetened fruit juice

Empty a jar of baby food into a measuring cup. Add unsweetened fruit juice to make 1 cup. Stir well and pour into a four-section lolly mould. Insert handles and freeze until set. To double the recipe, add another cup of juice.

Peanut Butter Sculptures

I don't know which part of this activity children enjoy more: building the sculpture or eating it!

Peanut butter
Crackers
Small plastic knife or lolly stick

Put peanut butter on a small plate or in a small plastic container (unless you don't mind your toddler sticking his fingers into the whole jar). If your child has an allergy to peanut butter, use cheese spread, cream cheese, jam, or honey. Show your child how to spread the peanut butter onto a cracker, then stick another cracker on top of it. Use a few different kinds of crackers if possible. Even animal crackers are fun.

Bananas, Honey, & Wheat Germ

This is a sticky activity but a banana lover's delight!

Banana
Honey
Milk
Wheat germ
Plastic knives or lolly sticks

Mix some honey with a little milk to thin it, then put it in a small bowl. Put some wheat germ in a second small bowl. Cut a banana in half and give your child a half to peel. Let him cut his banana half into smaller pieces with a plastic knife or lolly stick. Show him how to dip a banana chunk first into the honey bowl, then into the wheat germ. He may want to eat it right away, or you can place each dipped chunk on a small plate to save for later.

Painted Toast

2 tablespoons milk
Food colouring
Clean paintbrush
White bread
Toaster

Mix the milk with a few drops of food colouring in a small container. Use a paintbrush to paint designs or faces on the bread. Then toast the bread, butter it and eat it, or use it to make a sandwich.

'i Made it All By Myself' Cake

This is the type of cake about which even a very young child can boast, 'I made it all by myself'.

> 500g can crushed pineapple
> 450g can cherry pie filling
> Sponge cake mix
> ¾ cup butter or margarine

Butter a 9-inch by 13-inch baking tin. Dump in the crushed pineapple, including the juice and spread evenly. Spoon the cherry pie filling evenly over the pineapple. Sprinkle the yellow sponge cake mix over the fruit. Slice the butter or margarine thinly and place the pieces on top of the cake mix. Bake at 180C/350F/Gas mark 3 for 45 minutes.

Washing Vegetables

> Small basin of water
> Vegetable brush or dishcloth
> Vegetables or fruit to wash
> Tea towel for drying

Fill a small basin with several inches of water. Give your child several pieces of fruit or vegetables to wash in the basin. He may enjoy using a vegetable brush or gently rubbing them with a dishcloth. When they are clean, show him how to dry the fruit or vegetables with a clean tea towel.

Apple Shake-Ups

Apple
Knife
Sugar
Cinnamon
Ziploc bag

Peel an apple and cut it into toddler-size pieces. Or cut it into larger slices and have your older toddler use a plastic knife to cut it into smaller pieces. Place 1–2 tablespoons of sugar and about ½ teaspoon of cinnamon into a Ziploc bag. Add a few apple pieces, seal the bag and shake to coat the apples. Remove the coated apples from the bag and eat.

Fruit Salad

Younger toddlers can help cut the bananas and perhaps the canned fruit with a plastic knife. They can also put the ingredients in and mix them. Older toddlers can do most of the cutting with a dull knife. This recipe makes enough salad for a group of toddlers, so adjust the quantities as needed.

Canned peaches
Canned pears
Canned pineapple
Bananas
Apples
Natural or vanilla yogurt

Open the canned fruit and cut pieces small enough for toddlers to eat. Peel and slice bananas and apples. Mix it all in a large bowl with natural or vanilla yogurt and serve to toddlers in small bowls.

Zoo Sandwiches

Sliced bread
Cream cheese
Cream
Food colouring (optional)
Plastic knives
Animal biscuit cutters

Combine cream cheese with cream in a mixing bowl (1 tablespoon of cream per 3 ounces of cream cheese). Mix with a spoon until the cream cheese is soft. Add a few drops of food colouring, if desired and stir well. Cut bread in animal shapes with the biscuit cutters. Use a small plastic knife or lolly stick to spread the cream cheese mixture on the bread. If your child is not fond of cream cheese, use peanut butter, honey, or jam instead.

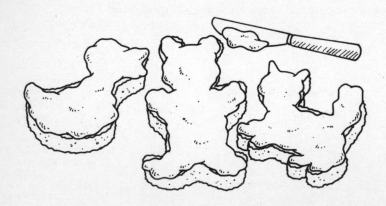

Quickie Biscuits

These biscuits aren't very nutritious, but older toddlers can practically make them on their own. There's no measuring if you use premeasured margarine squares and cleaning up is a breeze with only a bowl, mixing spoon and biscuit sheets.

1 package cake mix
½ cup butter or margarine
1 egg

Mix all the ingredients in a medium-size bowl. Mould into balls and place on greased baking trays. Bake at 180C/350F/Gas mark 3 for about 10 minutes or until done. Cool for a few minutes on the baking tray, then remove to a cooling rack to cool completely.

CHAPTER 4
Water Play

'A lot of people assume that because I am the mother of ten children, I must be an expert on motherhood, but such is not the case. It is true that I have learned a great deal over the years, but fortunately I have managed to forget most of what I have learned. (That is how I have remained sane.)'

–Teresa Bloomingdale

For young children, water isn't just for getting clean. In fact, water play for toddlers is rarely about getting clean. Dumping, pouring, filling, mixing, playing with sponges, corks, cups, bowls, soap, ice cubes and so on is a lot of fun for toddlers and preschoolers. It also encourages discovery and stimulates interest in the physical world.

Water play can also help parents and other care-givers maintain their sanity. During the early months of my third pregnancy, my two-year-old and one-year-old played happily in the bath on many rainy mornings. It was a great way for them to have fun while I did as little as possible!

Most toddlers probably have at least one waterplay session per day: bathtime. Here are a few suggestions to help your child get the maximum amount of fun out of every bath:

- Put a few inches of water in the tub, place your child in the water, then let the tap run slowly so your child can fill up cups, play in the stream of water and so on.

- Add as many plastic kitchen utensils as you can spare to your collection of bath toys.
- Sponges (plain or cut into shapes) are fun for the bath.
- Toddlers will love filling up small containers with water.
- Add inflated balloons, corks, or ice cubes to the bath. (Supervise carefully to prevent choking on small items or bits of broken balloon.)
- A ping-pong ball is lots of fun in the tub. Try to keep it under the water – it will always pop up!
- Poke a few holes in the bottom of a plastic container. Children will enjoy filling it with water and watching the water drip and dribble out of the bottom.

If your toddler is like mine, she loves to line up her little cups and other containers along the edge of the bathtub and then repeatedly fill them up, empty them out and fill them up again. While great fun for children, this activity usually results in a lot of water on the bathroom floor (and, in some cases, a lot of water leaking through to the ceiling of the room below). A small, Rubbermaid-type step stool placed in the bathtub gives your child a great platform for her containers and helps keep most of the water in the tub.

Water play is also a great kitchen activity. Most toddlers will enjoy standing on a chair at the kitchen sink and playing in a sinkful of water with bowls, cups and other containers. If you have a dishwasher in your kitchen, the open door of a clean, empty dishwasher makes a great water play table for your toddler. Simply add a bucket of water and some small cups and containers to fill and dump. A thick towel in front of the sink or under the open dishwasher door will help soak up spills.

The following ideas for water play cover a variety of situations-both indoors and out. You may find some of these ideas better suited to older toddlers and preschoolers. Remember: drowning in a waterfilled bucket or a few inches of water in the bathtub is a very real possibility for toddlers, so please supervise any water play carefully.

Cork Race

You will need one of each of the following items for each player. Many toddlers haven't yet mastered the skill of blowing through a straw, so you may want to save this idea for when your child is a little older.

> *Cork*
> *9-inch by 13-inch baking trays*
> *Straw*

Fill each baking pan with water and place the pans on a table or on the floor. Give each player a cork and a straw. The winner is the first one to blow her cork from one side of the pan to the other.

Wash the Floor

Sponge

Give your child a wet sponge and let her help you when you're washing the floor. Once you know she will not automatically empty it out on the floor, give her an inch or two of water in a small bucket or bowl. She will have fun being your helper and cleaning up is easy!

Michelangelo's Bathroom

Try this idea if your child hates getting water on her face when you wash her hair.

Colourful pictures
Tape

Tape some colourful pictures to the ceiling over your bathtub. (Old calendars are a great source for these.) Your child can look at the pictures and talk with you about them as you wash her hair. Unless she has a favourite, change the pictures often to maintain interest.

Fun with Water

If you don't mind water all over the floor, you can use this idea inside. Otherwise, you may want to save it for a warm day outdoors. Young toddlers tend to have more fun emptying the bucket rather than playing with the dishes and utensils, so try using a bucket that, when filled, is too heavy for a toddler to lift.

Large plastic basin or bucket
Various kitchen utensils: spoons, eggbeater, whisk and so on
Plastic bowls and dishes
Small plastic bottles
Funnel

Fill a basin or plastic bucket with warm water and let your child play with spoons, a whisk, an eggbeater and plastic bowls and dishes while you work. Show her how to use a funnel to fill a small plastic drinks bottle. If playing indoors, a thick towel or an old sheet placed under the basin or bucket will make cleanup a little easier.

Waterfall Game

Coins
Bowl, cup, or other container
Water

Fill a container almost to the top with water. Give each player a supply of coins. Take turns dropping a coin into the container. The game ends when one player drops in the coin that makes the water overflow.

Soap Crayons

These are fun to write with in the tub or to use when washing little hands.

1½ cup pure soap powder
Food colouring
½ cup water
Small containers or ice cube tray

Mix water and soap powder together. Add enough food colouring to get the colour you want. If you'd like more than one colour, divide the mixure into two or three small containers before adding food colouring. Pour the coloured soap into a small container (empty plastic film canisters work well) or an ice cube tray, or mould it into crayon shapes and let harden before using.

Drown the Coin

Paper towel
Glass filled with water
Pencil
Rubber band
Coin

Place the paper towel over the waterfilled glass. Wrap a rubber band around the top of the glass to hold the paper towel in place. Place the coin on the paper towel in the centre of the glass. Take turns poking holes in the paper towel with the pencil. The game ends when someone drowns the coin by poking the hole that finally makes the coin sink to the bottom of the glass.

Bathtub Soap Paint

You may want to skip this idea if your child has sensitive skin.

½ cup pure soap flakes
¾ cup water
Food colouring
Electric mixer or wire whisk
Paintbrush
Spray bottle

Use an electric mixer or wire whisk to whip the soap flakes and water together until you get the texture of shaving cream. Add food colouring (be careful–it can stain the grout around ceramic tiles and should be omitted if this worries you). Use a brush to paint the wall around the bathtub. Give your child a spray bottle filled with water and let her spray the paint off.

Water Balloon Catch

Balloons
Water

Fill several balloons with water and play catch with them, or use pavement chalk to draw a target on the pavement and aim for that instead.

Water Play

This bathtime variation is great for long, rainy days.

Plastic baby bathtub
Bath toys

Sit your child in an empty bathtub with just a nappy on. Fill a plastic baby bathtub or other large container with water and set it beside your child. Provide an assortment of bath toys that she can play with. (Cups, spoons, bowls, funnels, empty squeeze bottles, a plastic teapot and sponges all make excellent water play toys.)

Bathtime Bubbles

Bubble solution
Bubble blower

Blow bubbles for your child while she sits in the bath. Have her try to catch them in her open hands or clap her hands together to pop them.

Coloured ice Cubes

Ice cubes will melt fairly quickly in a warm bath, but they can still be a choking hazard for little ones. Please supervise carefully.

Ice cube tray
Water
Food colouring

Make coloured ice cubes by adding a drop of food colouring to the water in each section of an ice cube tray. Freeze. Add a bowl of different-coloured ice cubes to the bath for some bath-time fun.

Sponge Play

Sponges
Water
2 bowls or other containers

Fill one bowl with water and add a few drops of food colouring if you like. Show your toddler how to place the sponge in the bowl of water, then transfer the water to the empty bowl by squeezing the sponge.

Ice Blocks

If small ice cubes melt too quickly, try making a larger block of ice to play with in the bath or outside on a warm summer day.

Clean milk carton
Water
Food colouring (optional)
Small plastic toys (optional)

Make an ice block by freezing water in a clean milk carton. If you like, add a few drops of food colouring to the water before freezing, or drop in a few small plastic toys. Your child will enjoy playing with the block in the bath or outside in the pool. If you've frozen small plastic toys inside the block, watch your child's surprise as the ice melts and the toys appear.

As a variation, fill balloons with water, tie tightly and freeze to make ice balls.

Toddler Sprinkler

This idea may become a real hit around your house – outside, of course!

> *Large plastic bottle (large plastic milk bottles work brilliantly)*
> *Hammer and nail*

Use a hammer and nail to poke holes in the bottom of a large plastic bottle. When you're outside, fill the bottle with water and let your child sprinkle the grass, flowers, pavement, driveway and so on.

Baster Play

In *The Preschooler's Busy Book*, I suggest this activity using an eyedropper. Toddlers will enjoy doing the same with a large baster.

> *Kitchen baster*
> *Plastic bowls or other containers*
> *Water*

Fill one bowl with water and add a few drops of food colouring if you like. Show your toddler how to place the baster in the bowl full of water and squeeze the bulb. She will enjoy watching the tube fill up with water. Show her how to hold the baster over an empty container and let go of the bulb to release the water.

Rock Drop

Paddling pool, large bucket or dishpan
Water
Rocks large enough to pass the choke test

Put a few inches of water in a paddling pool, large bucket, or dishpan and let your toddler drop the rocks into the water.

Water Rhythms

A toddler with a hose will have a good time, no doubt about it. Upside-down pots add a dimension of sound for some extra fun.

Metal pots and lids
Garden hose with spray attachment

Turn the pots upside down on the grass or driveway. Prop up some of the pot lids against a wall or fence. Turn on the water and let your toddler spray the pots and lids to hear the drumming noises.

Ball Splash

Paddling pool
Water
Large beach ball

Fill a paddling pool with a few inches of water. Face your toddler across the pool and take turns throwing a beach ball hard at the water, trying to splash each other and yourself.

Ice Play

This is a great outdoor idea for a hot day. If you'd rather do this inside, sit your toddler in an empty bathtub with the pan of ice beside her.

Crushed ice
Plastic basin or large bowl
Bath toys

Put some crushed ice into a plastic basin or large plastic bowl. Your child will have fun using her bath toys (cups, spoons, bowls and so on) to play with the ice. If you're making the ice instead of buying it, add a few drops of food colouring to the water before freezing it.

Target Practise

This is a great game for a summer get-together or birthday party. If your child isn't old enough to shoot a squirt gun, try using the garden hose instead.

Large plastic drink bottles
Ping-pong balls
Squirt gun or garden hose

Fill three or four plastic drinks bottles with water. Set the bottles on a level surface. (A child's picnic table works well.) Place a ping-pong ball on top of each bottle. Use the squirt gun or garden hose to try to shoot the balls off the bottles.

Sponge Tag

Sponges
Bucket of water

Soak sponges in water, then have fun throwing them at each other. If your child doesn't like the idea of being the target, try throwing sponges at a tree or garage door, or use pavement chalk to draw a big circle or other shapes and aim for that instead.

Coloured Sand

Spray bottle
Water
Food colouring or liquid paint

Fill a spray bottle with water and add a few drops of food colouring or a few spoonfuls of liquid paint. Let your child spray the sand in the sandbox to make a colourful desert. Turn the sand over with a shovel and watch the colour disappear. Now your child can start all over again.

Car Wash

Bucket of warm, soapy water
Cloth or sponge
Hose
Riding toys (miniature cars, tractors)

Help your child set up a toddler car wash. Give her a bucket of warm, soapy water and a cloth or sponge and let her wash her riding toys. She may need help using the hose to rinse them when she's finished.

Gone Fishing

Large bucket or dishpan
Water
Plastic worm lures (without hooks)
Scoop or small strainer (optional)
Corks, ping-pong balls, or small sponge scraps (optional)

Fill a large bucket or dishpan with water. Add a few plastic worm lures and let your toddler have fun trying to catch them in her hands or in a scoop or small strainer. For variety, float corks, ping-pong balls, or small sponge scraps in the water. Encourage your toddler to scoop them out one by one.

Funnels and Tubes

12-to 18-inch length of flexible plastic tubing, ½ inch in diameter
Funnel
Plastic measuring cup or small container
Large bucket or saucepan
Food colouring

Fill the large bucket or saucepan with water. Add a few drops of food colouring to make coloured water. Attach a funnel to one end of the flexible plastic tubing. (If it doesn't stay securely, you may want to use a glue gun to permanently join the two.) Place the other end of the tubing in the bucket or saucepan.

Show your toddler how to scoop up some water from the bucket and pour it into the funnel. She will enjoy watching the coloured water flow through the tubing and back into the bucket. If you like, use two buckets and have her transfer water from one bucket to another with her cup, funnel and tubing.

CHAPTER 5
Outdoor Adventures

'As soon as I stepped out of my mother's womb on to dry land, I realized that I had made a mistake, that I shouldn't have come, but the trouble with children is that they are not returnable.'

–Quentin Crisp

Outdoor play every day, in almost any weather, is essential for children of all ages. Whether playing in the snow, picking spring flowers, crunching autumn leaves, or stomping in puddles after a rain, toddlers need to be outdoors to master their newfound skills of walking, running, climbing and jumping.

Whatever the weather, toddlers will almost certainly find something with which to amuse themselves. Most never tire of sand and water play and swings and slides are a great deal of fun as well as a great way to work off some of their seemingly endless energy. Whether you push a stroller, pull a wagon, or walk with your child at a toddler's pace, both parent and child will benefit from short walks outdoors almost every day.

The ideas in this chapter will provide some fun and interesting things to do with your toddler outdoors. Most require a minimum of materials and you will find that with minor changes, most are suitable for any season and any weather. Many indoorplay ideas in Chapter 2 and water-play ideas in Chapter 4 are also easily adaptable to outdoor play.

Measuring Magic

Measuring cups and spoons
Bowls or small containers
Water, sand, or mud

Give your child an assortment of cups, spoons, bowls and other containers and let him play outdoors with water, sand, or mud.

Spaghetti Splash

We tried this in our backyard one warm summer day as part of our playgroup windup. After many years have passed, my children and the parents who attended still talk about it! Watch out, though, it can kill the grass!

2–3 packages cooked spaghetti
⅓ cup vegetable oil
Food colouring
Child's paddling pool

Mix the ingredients in a child's paddling pool. Children may want to play with the spaghetti with their hands, sit in it, or (as we tried) use a small slide to get right into the middle of it.

Mud Handprints

Mud
Sturdy paper or plastic plate
Spatula or knife for smoothing

Fill the plate with thick mud and smooth into a flat, even surface. Have your child press his open hand into the mud and remove. Place the mud in the sun to dry. This won't last, but it's fun to look at for a while. For lasting prints, use plaster of Paris.

Bubble Solutions

The following three bubble solution recipes come from Science World in Vancouver, British Columbia. They say the following about glycerine: 'Not all detergents require the addition of glycerine in order to make good soap solutions. Glycerine helps soap bubbles hold water and this helps to keep the bubbles from popping. Try a tablespoon or two for a small batch (we're not exact about it). Glycerine can be purchased at most pharmacies. You won't need much, so don't go buying caseloads.'

All-Purpose Bubble Solution

Here's a good all-purpose solution for most bubble tricks, experiments and activities.

7–10 parts water
1 part washing-up liquid
Glycerine

Combine water, detergent and 1–2 tablespoons of glycerine (see note above) in a bowl or plastic container.

Thick Bubble Solution

This is a thick, gloopy solution that forms bubbles strong enough to withstand a small puff of air. You can blow bubbles inside of bubbles with this mixture and you don't need a straw. Just make a bubble and blow!

> 2½–3 parts water
> 1 part washing-up liquid
> Glycerine

Combine water, detergent and 1–2 tablespoons of glycerine (see note above) in a bowl or plastic container.

Bouncy Bubble Solution

This is a fun solution that you can bounce off your clothes.

> 2 packages unflavoured gelatin
> 4 cups hot water (just boiled)
> 3–5 tablespoons glycerine
> 3 tablespoons washing-up liquid

Dissolve the gelatin in hot water. Add glycerine and washing-up liquid. This mixture will gel, so you'll need to reheat it whenever you use it.

Bubble Fun

Plastic drinking straws

Shop-bought or homemade bubble solution (see Bubble

Solutions on page 127)

Scissors

Tape

Make a bubble wand by cutting two plastic drinking straws in half, then taping the four pieces together. Blowing through the straws will send lots of tiny bubbles in many directions.

Jelly Jumping

4 large packages jelly
Baby bathtub

Prepare jelly according to package directions. Place it in a baby's bathtub or small basin and let your child stand in it, sit in it, run his fingers through it or paint with it.

Frog in the Grass

4 green rubber frogs (or rubber snakes, beanbags,
or small plastic toys)

Have your child stand on the far side of the yard and close his eyes. Hide the frogs in the grass in different spots around the yard. When you yell 'Frog in the grass!' your child must run and find the frogs. Make sure he grabs them before they hop away!

Red, Red, Red

You can play this game with a group of children or when it's just you
and your child.

Have the players stand next to each other behind a starting line. The
leader calls out three colours (for example, 'Red, red, red!'). If the colours
don't match ('Red, red, yellow!'), no one moves. If the colours do match,
then children run, skip, or hop to a distant point and back. Feel free to
substitute animals ('Cat, cat, dog!'), body parts ('Hand, hand, foot!'), or
whatever you like.

Leaf Scrunch

Dry leaves
Small box
Contact paper

Collect dry leaves in a bag on an autumn walk with your child. At home,
put the leaves into a box and let your child scrunch the leaves with his
hands. Use some of the colourful pieces to make an autumn collage on
a piece of clear contact paper.

Balloon Kites

Flying a kite is difficult and frustrating for toddlers and preschoolers. These 'kites' are guaranteed to fly, even on days with light wind.

Large, round helium balloons
Kite string
Paper streamers (optional)

Tie one end of a long length of kite string to a round helium balloon and the other to your child's wrist. He will find it fun and easy to fly his balloon and you won't worry about crashes and tangles. Try attaching lengths of paper streamers to the balloon to give it a more authentic kite look.

Dodge Ball

This is a fun game for four or more children.

Large, soft ball (try crumpled up newspaper and tape, or onion-bag netting stuffed with cotton balls)

Have children form a circle with one child in the middle. Each player in the outer circle takes a turn throwing the ball at the child in the middle, who tries to dodge out of the way. When the child in the middle gets hit, he changes places with the child who hit him.

Toddler Ball

Plastic ball
Plastic bat and tee (optional)

Show your child how to throw or kick a plastic ball, or have him try hitting it with a plastic bat off a tee. Pick up the ball and chase your child to a 'base' (a tree or other designated point) and then back to 'home'. You may want to tag your child occasionally, but let him be 'safe' sometimes, too.

Shadow Tracing

Chalk

Go outside with your child on a sunny day. If your child will stand still long enough, trace his shadow on the pavement or driveway. Have him change positions, then trace his shadow again. Make several tracings, then see if your child can fit his shadow back inside the tracings.

For a fun alternative, trace his shadow on a big sheet of newsprint or other paper. Let him fingerpaint his shadow or colour it with crayons or markers.

Digging for Treasure

Small objects to hide
Shovels
Colander
Sandbox

Hide small objects in the sandbox for your toddler to find as he digs about. Try using an old kitchen colander to sift through the sand. If you like, spraypaint rocks in shiny silver and gold and show your toddler how to search for hidden treasure.

Nature Bracelet

Masking tape
Scissors

Before going outdoors with your child, wrap a piece of masking tape to his wrist, sticky side up. As you explore, help him attach colourful leaves, flowers and other interesting discoveries to his bracelet. When done, use scissors to snip off the nature bracelet. Display on a bulletin board, shelf, or wall.

Changing Colours

This is a good activity for outdoors or in and will also entertain children on a long car ride.

Coloured cellophane in various colours

Give your child a piece of coloured cellophane. Go for a walk outside and encourage your child to look at familiar objects through the cellophane. Your child will enjoy seeing how the colour of everyday objects changes when seen through the cellophane. If you like, change the colour of cellophane your child is using, or look through two pieces of cellophane at once to see how the colours change yet again.

Teddy Swing

Rope, heavy string, or ribbon
Teddy bear or favourite stuffed animal

Tie one end of a length of rope, heavy string, or ribbon around the waist of your child's favourite teddy bear or other stuffed animal. Tie the other end of the rope to a tree branch so that teddy is about 2 feet off the ground. Your child will have fun pushing his teddy to make him swing.

Crayon Slide

If you have a slide in your backyard (or a small one indoors), this activity will add a new dimension to sliding fun.

Slide
Newsprint paper or long length of paper
Tape
Crayons

Tape a length of newsprint paper to your child's slide. Give him one or two crayons (perhaps one for each hand) and have him slide down the slide, holding the crayons to the paper as he goes. He will enjoy seeing the squiggly lines and designs he's made. Change colours and keep sliding until your child tires of this activity.

If you like, bundle up three or four (or more) crayons with a rubber band for a different effect.

Window Painting

Fingerpaint
Washing-up liquid (optional)
Wet paintbrush or cotton bud (optional)

Adding a little washing-up liquid to the fingerpaint makes cleaning up easier! On a warm day outdoors, let your child fingerpaint on the outside of a glass patio door or low window. When the paint dries, use a wet paintbrush or cotton bud dipped in water to make a design on the paint. Cleaning up with a sponge and bucket of water or garden hose can be part of the fun.

Rope Games

This activity is good for either indoor or outdoor play.

Long rope

Lay a long rope in a zigzag pattern in the grass or on your deck. See if your child can walk on the rope. Lay the rope in a straight line like a tightrope and have your child hold out his arms to balance himself as he walks. With the rope still lying straight, ask your child to think of how many ways he can go over it: walk across it, hop over it (on one or two feet), jump across it, crawl across it, or any other way he can think of.

CHAPTER 6
Out and About

'Children are a great comfort in your old age and they help you reach it faster, too.'

–Lionel M. Kauffman

Most children, no matter what their age, would rather be playing and moving about than sitting still for an extended period of time. Also, toddlers are fairly limited in their language skills and ability to play games and carry out independent activities. For these reasons, long car rides and waits at the doctor's can be especially frustrating for those with a toddler in tow.

There are, however, simple things you can do to help your child through these challenging situations. Provide her with her very own Busy Bag (see Chapter 1) and fill it with toddler appropriate items. Bring along her favourite book, toy, or snack to help her through times when you're forced to sit and wait. Sing songs, recite nursery rhymes and learn some simple finger plays to keep her attention (see Chapter 7).

The ideas in this chapter are great for those times when your toddler just has to sit. The simple games and activities will help keep her entertained and happy and many may become favourites for other times as well.

Where is it?

As you're driving in the car, name things that you see and ask your toddler to point to them (for example, 'Where is the tree?') If you're waiting in a place where your child can move around, ask her to walk over to the object you name.

Colour of the Day

Before you set out on a car trip, choose a 'Colour of the Day'. As you're driving in the car, shopping at the supermarket, or waiting at the doctor's, help your toddler point to and identify all the things she sees that match the colour you've chosen.

What Would You Be?

You can encourage your older two or three-year-old to use her imagination by playing games such as this. Ask your child, 'If you could spend one day as an animal, which one would you be?' and 'What do you think your day might be like?' You may want to give your child some examples or start the game off yourself, pretending to be a dog digging for a bone, or a baby bird in the nest waiting for mummy to return.

Car Book

Old magazines
Scissors
Paper card
Glue
Clear contact paper
Hole punch
Ribbon

Look through old magazines for pictures of cars or other vehicles. Cut out the pictures and glue them to pieces of paper card. Protect the pages by covering them with clear contact paper. Punch two or three holes in the left margin of each page, then thread ribbon through the holes to make a book. (If you like, use a ring binder or staple the pages together.)

Give your child her car book to look through as you drive along. Ask her questions as she looks at the pages. For example, 'Can you find a blue car?' or 'Can you find a truck?' and so on.

Nursery Rhyme Fun

As you drive along, recite a familiar nursery rhyme or sing a familiar song to your child. When you get to a rhyming word, stop and see if your toddler can say or sing the correct word. For example, say, 'Hickory, dickory, dock, the mouse ran up the _____' or 'Little Jack Horner sat in a _____' or 'Jack, be nimble, Jack be quick, Jack jump over the _____'.

Ask a Question

While riding in the car or waiting for your meal at a restaurant, take a few minutes to ask your child some questions. Try to avoid yes/no questions and encourage your child to give reasons for her answers. Some of her responses may be hilarious, but you'll be surprised at what you can learn about your child if you take the time to really listen to the answers she gives. Here are a few questions to start you off:

- Who is your best friend?
- Where does money come from?
- What is the best thing about Daddy (or Mummy)?
- What is the nicest thing that has ever happened to you?
- What is your favourite thing to do?
- When does God sleep?

Stop and Go

Red and green paper card
Scissors
Tape
Straw

Cut two circles from the red and green paper card. Tape a straw to the back of each circle, leaving enough straw extending below the circle for your child to hold on to. Give your child the circles to hold in the car.

As you drive up to a red light, say to your child, 'I'm stopping now because the light is red. Can you hold up your red light?' When the light turns green, say, 'I'm starting to drive now because the light is green. Can you hold up your green light?' If you like, refer to your child's red and green lights as red and green circles to reinforce the concept of shape.

You can also play this game by cutting a stop sign from red paper card. Tape a straw to the back, give it to your child and ask her to hold her sign up every time you stop.

Toddler Photo Album

This little homemade photo album slips easily into a bag and comes in handy during long car rides or waits in a restaurant or at the doctor's.

Photos of friends, family, pets and your toddler
Paper card
Glue
Clear contact paper
Scissors
Hole punch
Ribbon

Glue photos of your child and her friends, family and pets to pieces of paper card. Cover them with clear contact paper and cut to size, leaving a border of at least ½ inch around the photo. Punch two holes in the left margin of each page. Thread ribbon through the holes to make a photo album. Your child will enjoy looking at this over and over.

If you like, use a small bought photo album (one photo per page) instead of making one with cardboard and contact paper.

Shopping List

This word game may be beyond most one and two-year-olds, but older two and three-year-olds will love it.

As you drive along, say to your child, 'I went to the shop and I bought carrots, cabbage and cream. What else did I buy?' Your child must add items to your shopping list that begin with the same sound as the items you have named. You can tell your child the rule for adding items (that they must begin with the same sound), or let older children figure it out for themselves.

If they try to add something that doesn't begin with the same sound, tell them, 'No, that wasn't on my list.' They'll probably guess the rule after a few tries, but if they have trouble, keep adding items to your list until they understand.

What Would Happen if ...?

This is a great activity to promote creative thinking in young children. Ask your child some 'What would happen if ...' questions. For example, 'What would happen if the dinosaurs came back?' or 'What would happen if cars could fly?' or 'What would happen if broccoli tasted like chocolate?' or 'What would happen if all the trees were red?' and so on.

Out and About ────────────────────────────

Felt Faces

Cardboard
Scissors
Felt
Glue Pen or marker
Ziploc bag, or small shoebox for storage

Cut several oval shapes out of cardboard. Trace around these shapes on pieces of felt (since these will be faces, felt in a variety of skin colours is desirable, but brightly coloured felt will work, too). Cut out the felt shapes you have traced and glue them to the cardboard ovals. Cut additional facial features from the felt in a variety of colours. These features should include eyes, noses, mouths (smiling and frowning), ears (with and without earrings, if you like) and hair. Older children may enjoy using additional features such as eyebrows, eyeglasses, moustaches and so on.

Place the felt pieces (oval face shapes and facial features) in a Ziploc bag, or small shoebox. This makes a clean and quiet take-along game to play in the car or while you're waiting.

Sandpaper Play

This is a clean, quiet activity that travels well. Store sandpaper and wool in a Ziploc bag and have it handy for a long car ride or whenever you need something quick for your child to do.

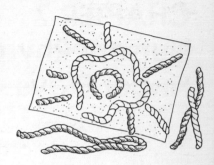

Coarse sandpaper
Wool in various colours

Cut various colours of wool into different lengths. Show your toddler how the wool sticks to the sandpaper. She will enjoy creating a design, pulling it off and starting over again.

Take-Along Tape

Tape recorder with microphone
Cassette tape

Spend some time on your own making a tape for your toddler. Include familiar household sounds, sounds of animals, outdoor sounds, voices that the child will recognise and so on. As you drive along, play the tape for your toddler and ask her to guess the sounds she hears. As a variation, choose a story that your child is familiar with and read it on tape. As you read, make some mistakes, changing words in obvious places throughout the story. Have your child listen to the tape and pick out the errors.

CHAPTER 7
Nursery Rhymes and
Finger Plays

'There never was a child so lovely but his mother was glad to get him asleep.'

– Ralph Waldo Emerson

Nursery rhymes and finger plays can be used in many different circumstances. You can use them on walks with your toddler or driving in the car. They will amuse your child at changing time or while he waits for his meal in his highchair. Sing or say the rhymes and finger plays as you rock in the rocking chair or as your child plays in his bath. Nursery rhymes and finger plays are appropriate just about anytime and anyplace.

To help you learn the words of any song or rhyme you're not familiar with, begin by reciting two lines at a time, repeating those lines throughout the day until you know them by heart. Add another two lines and continue in this way until the whole rhyme is memorised. Posting one or two unfamiliar rhymes around your baby's change table, or on the kitchen wall close to his highchair will also help you learn them. You'll know them well after reading and saying them to your toddler several times.

Slowly, Slowly

Use your hands to mime the actions suggested by the words, or just use
the rhyme as a tickling game with baby.

Slowly, slowly, very slowly
Creeps the garden snail.
Slowly, slowly, very slowly
Up the wooden rail.

Quickly, quickly, very quickly
Runs the little mouse.
Quickly, quickly, very quickly
Round about the house.

Snowflakes

Mime the actions suggested by the words.

Softly, softly falling so,
This is how the snowflakes go.
Pitter-patter, pitter-patter,
Pit pit pat,
Down go the raindrops
On my hat.

Granny's Glasses

Make appropriate actions to fit the words as you say them. For glasses, join the thumb and forefinger on each hand. Use a higher voice for Granny, a deeper voice for Grandad.

These are Granny's glasses,
This is Granny's hat;
Granny claps her hands like this,
And folds them in her lap.

These are Grandad's glasses,
This is Grandad's hat;
This is the way he folds his arms,
And has a little nap.

Mix a Pancake

Mime each action as you say it.

Mix a pancake,
Stir a pancake,
Pop it in the pan.
Fry the pancake,
Toss the pancake,
Catch it if you can!

Two Little Eyes

Point to each feature as it is mentioned.

Two little eyes to look around,
Two little ears to hear each sound,
One little nose to smell what's sweet,
One little mouth that likes to eat.

Here's a Ball for Baby

Here's a ball for baby, (Make a ball with cupped hands.)
Big and soft and round.
Here is baby's hammer, (Hammer with one fist.)
See how he can pound.

Here is baby's music, (Clap hands.)
Clapping, clapping, so.
Here are baby's soldiers, (Hold fingers up straight.)
Standing in a row.

Here is his umbrella, (Hold hands above head.)
To keep our baby dry.
Here is baby's cradle, (Fold arms together and rock them.)
To rock-a-baby-bye.

i Hear Thunder

This is sung to the tune of 'Frère Jacques,' or 'Are You Sleeping?'

I hear thunder, I hear thunder, (Drum feet on the floor.)
Hark, don't you, hark, don't you? (Pretend to listen.)
Pitterpatter raindrops, (Flutter your fingers for raindrops.)

Pitterpatter raindrops,
I'm wet through, (Shake your body vigorously.)
So are you! (Point to your child.)

Ten Little Gentlemen

Use your fingers to represent the gentlemen in this rhyme. When the door closes at the end, be sure to give a big clap.

Ten little gentlemen, standing in a row.
Bow, little gentlemen, bow down low;
Walk, little gentlemen, right across the floor,
And don't forget, gentlemen, to please close the door.

Five Little Monkeys

Mime the actions of each monkey and use your fingers to indicate the number of monkeys as you say this rhyme.

Five little monkeys walked along the shore;
One went a-sailing,
Then there were four.

Four little monkeys climbed up a tree;
One of them tumbled down,
Then there were three.

Three little monkeys found a pot of glue;
One got stuck in it,
Then there were two.

Two little monkeys found a currant bun;
One ran away with it,
Then there was one.

One little monkey cried all afternoon,
So they put him in an airplane
And sent him to the moon.

Walking through the Jungle

Pretend to walk very carefully through the jungle and mime the actions to suggest each animal. It's easy to make up more verses for this rhyme.

Walking through the jungle,
What did I see?
A big lion roaring
At me, me, me!

Walking through the jungle,
What did I see?
A baby monkey laughing
At me, me, me!

Walking through the jungle,
What did I see?
A slippery snake hissing
At me, me, me!

Five Little Mice

Use the fingers of one hand for the mice and the other hand for the cat. Continue each verse with one less mouse until there are no little mice scampering back.

Five little mice came out to play,
Gathering up crumbs on their way;
Out came a pussycat, sleek and black
Four little mice went scampering back.

Four little mice came out to play ...

Little Pussycats

One, two, three, four, *(Hold up four fingers from the right hand and count them.)*
These little pussycats came to my door.
They just stood there and said 'Good day,' *(Make the fingers bow on 'Good day.')*
And then they tiptoed right away. *(Walk the fingers away over the front of the body and behind the left shoulder.)*

CHAPTER 8
Early Learning Fun

'Before I got married I had six theories about bringing up children. Now I have six children and no theories.'

– Lord Rochester

Children are learning all the time. Toddlers learn with their hands, their ears, their noses, their mouths and their feet. They learn by doing, looking, touching, smelling, tasting, banging, dropping and listening. A toddler's play is her pathway to learning. Seen in that light, most of the activities in this book provide learning opportunities for toddlers: building with blocks; playing with mud, sand and water; swinging, sliding and running outdoors; moving to music; and crafting with paper, paints and glue. All these activities help your child learn and help her make sense of the world around her.

The best way to optimise your child's ability to learn is to create a stimulating environment for her. Provide her with lots of exposure to interesting things to see, touch and hear. Recite rhymes, sing and play finger games as you change her nappy (post one or two new rhymes or songs by the changing table to help you learn them). Look through magazines for colourful pictures of everyday objects; paste them onto cardboard, cover them with clear contact paper and display them on the wall by the cot, changing table, or highchair. And most importantly, talk, talk, talk to your child about everything you're doing.

Don't be in a rush to push academic learning. Young children – toddlers in particular – must spend lots of time developing their motor skills in order to make academic learning possible and productive. Activities that develop gross motor skills include running, jumping, hopping, dancing and playing with balls, pull toys, push toys, riding toys, climbing toys, swings and slides. Activities that develop fine motor skills include filling and emptying boxes and containers and playing with nesting or stacking toys, simple wooden jigsaw puzzles, shape sorters and blocks. You'll find ideas for these types of activities throughout this book.

The activities in this chapter deal primarily with those skills we think of as 'academic': sorting, matching, classifying and recognising patterns, shapes, colours and so on. All these skills are required in order for a child to learn basic maths and reading skills. But your toddler can learn these skills in any number of ways. For instance, playing with Lego is a great way to learn basic maths skills: a toddler can sort pieces by colour and size, build towers and compare their sizes, count pieces, make patterns and so on. These are essential activities for maths readiness.

Many of the ideas in this chapter are not for everyone. Some will require a fair amount of time to prepare, making them more suitable for a day-care or preschool setting where more than one child will benefit. If you do choose to spend time assembling these activities, be sure to protect them as best you can. Covering with clear contact paper makes cards and other items more durable. Storage is also important. Shoeboxes are great for storage and they stack nicely on shelves or in cupboards. Sets of cards should be zipped into individual Ziploc bags and stored in a large plastic container with a cover. Sets of cards relating to similar concepts – colours or shapes, for example – should be stored together.

Can You Find Your Knee?

Most of us play this game informally with our children at one time or another. Very young children often easily point to their eyes, noses, mouths and ears when asked to do so. Encourage them to identify less common body parts including nostrils, eyelashes, fingernails, lips, throat, wrists, knees, ankles and so on. This will stimulate the development of memory and vocabulary as well as their ability to recognise parts of the body.

Animal Sort

Gather together all the stuffed animals you can find. Help your toddler sort them by colour or by size (using words like small, smaller, smallest, big, bigger and biggest). Older children may want to sort them by the type of sound they make (loud, soft) or by their habitat (jungle, forest, farm).

Pocket Matching

This is a fun game for toddlers, but takes a while to prepare.

Wrapping paper or fabric in 4-6 different patterns and colours

Scissors

Large piece of cardboard

Glue

Clear contact paper

Utility knife

Small index cards or pieces of cardboard or heavy paper

Cut a pocket from each piece of giftwrap. Glue the pockets to a large piece of cardboard, leaving the top of the pocket open. Cover the cardboard with clear contact paper. Slit open the top of each pocket with a utility knife. Cut wrapping paper rectangles that will fit in the pockets. (These will be the handkerchiefs.) Glue them to small index cards and cover both sides with clear contact paper. Your toddler will have fun matching the handkerchiefs to the pockets. Store the handkerchiefs in an envelope or Ziploc bag attached to the back of the cardboard.

Short and Tall

Paper towel rolls
Scissors
Colourful contact paper or wrapping paper (optional)

Cut paper towel rolls into several different sizes. If you like, cover them with colourful contact paper. Encourage your child to stand the rolls up in order from shortest to tallest. Store the rolls in an empty tin or shoebox when not in use.

Pompom Fun

Pompoms in various sizes and colours

Purchase pompoms in a variety of colours and sizes from a fabric or craft store. For very young children, start with no more than three colours or sizes. Use several sizes of pompoms in one colour and encourage your child to sort them by size. Use one size of pompom in several colours and ask your child to sort them by colour. Store pompoms in a Ziploc bag when not in use.

Spools of thread also work well for sorting and matching. Use two spools of each colour in at least three different colours.

Picture Box

This takes a bit of time to prepare. Try starting with just a few pictures and adding to your collection as time permits.

File or recipe box
Index cards to fit the box
Magazine pictures
Scissors
Glue
Clear contact paper

Cut interesting, colourful pictures of familiar objects from magazines. Glue them onto the index cards and cover with clear contact paper. Place the cards in the file or recipe box. Your toddler will enjoy looking at the pictures by herself or with you. If you use 4-inch by 6-inch index cards, they will fit in a small photo album, an easy item to slip into most bags. Take it with you on a long car ride, talking about each picture as you look at it.

You can maintain your Picture Box as your child grows, adding new pictures and perhaps dividing the pictures into categories such as flowers, animals, people and so on. Your Picture Box will eventually be a great sorting game, too.

Peg Colours

Spring-type clothes pegs
Paint (optional)
Coloured dot stickers (or use white and colour them yourself)
Empty tin

Paint five or six clothes pegs in different colours to match the coloured dot stickers, or decorate each peg with additional coloured dot stickers. Stick coloured dot stickers evenly around the top of the tin, leaving some space in between. Show your toddler how to clip each peg just above the matching coloured dot. Store the clothes pegs inside the tin when not in use.

Spoon Match

2 sets of measuring spoons

Mix up two sets of measuring spoons. Encourage your child to match up two spoons of the same size. Use only one set of spoons and have your child order them from smallest to largest.

Large and Small

5-6 pairs of objects that are similar in every way except size (adult/child socks, long/short pencils, dinner/lunch plates)

Holding up the two matching items, ask your child which one is smaller. Be sure to use terms such as bigger, smaller, shorter and longer in your everyday conversation to draw attention to the size of objects around you.

Picture Sort

If the cutting and gluing aspect of preparing this activity will take more time than you have, use two sets of matching stickers instead.

Metal lids
Double set of pictures (either photographs or from a magazine)
Glue
Clear contact paper
Magnets (optional)
Plastic container or shoebox

Cut a double set of pictures of family and friends (or pictures from two identical magazines) into a round shape that will fit the metal lid. Glue the pictures onto the lids and cover with clear contact paper. (You should have two sets of lids exactly the same.) Have your child sort the lids into pairs by matching the two pictures that are the same. If you like, glue magnets to the backs of the lids and make this a refrigerator activity.

Store the lids in a plastic container or shoebox with a slit cut in the top. Your toddler will enjoy dropping the lids into the opening to put the game away.

More Fun with Pictures

If you don't have any old calendars with appropriate pictures on hand, check out bookstores in January when they're selling calendars at big discounts. They're a great source of big, beautiful pictures in many different themes.

Old calendars with pictures of recognisable objects
(dogs, cats, cars and so on)
Paper card
Scissors
Glue
Clear contact paper

Cut out several pictures, mount them on paper card and cover with clear contact paper. If the pictures are a standard size, you can put them in a three ring binder; otherwise, store them in a box or file folder. Your child will love to look at the pictures. As she gets older, she'll enjoy mixing them up and sorting them out (all the dogs in one pile, cats in another and so on).

Pasta Sort

Dried pasta in 2–3 (or more) different shapes
Bowl or plastic container

Combine two or three different shapes of dried pasta in a bowl or plastic container. Pick out one piece and ask your toddler to find a piece that matches. If you like, have several small containers on hand and ask your toddler to sort the pasta into the containers. For colourful pasta, dye the pasta beforehand using the Pasta Dye recipe on page 305.

More Pompom Fun

Pompoms in various sizes and colours
Clear plastic drinking cups
Permanent marker

Use a permanent marker to make dots on the front of a clear plastic cup. One cup should have one dot, another two dots, the next three dots and so on. You can mark as many cups as you feel your child is able to match. Give her an assortment of pompoms and show her how to drop the same number of pompoms as dots into the cup. If you like, use beans, large nuts, golf tees, large plastic paper clips, small spools of thread or other small objects in place of pompoms. Store the cups and objects in a small box when not in use.

Parking Game

This simple matching game is lots of fun. Even toddlers with no concept of colour will enjoy parking the cars in the garages, whether they match or not.

Small boxes (shoeboxes work well, as do some cereal boxes)
3-4 toy cars in different colours
Scissors
Paper card
Glue
Paint (optional)
Coloured contact paper (optional)

In one side of each box cut a garage door big enough to fit a toy car. Cover each box with coloured paper card, matching the colours of the paper to the cars. (If you like, use coloured contact paper or paint the boxes instead.) Turn each box upside down so the bottom of the box is the roof of the garage. Encourage your child to park each car in the garage of the same colour. Store the garages and cars in a larger box or plastic container when not in use.

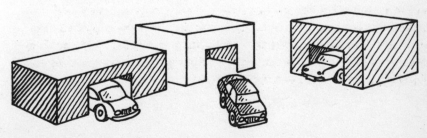

Find the Colour

Tell your child, 'I see the colour blue. Can you find it?' As you count down from ten to zero, your child must then run to touch something that includes the colour you have named before you finish counting.

Egg Sort

Even toddlers too young for sorting and matching activities will have fun playing with these colourful plastic eggs.

12 plastic Easter eggs
Glue gun
Egg carton

Purchase a dozen inexpensive plastic Easter eggs in three to six different colours. Use a glue gun to glue the two parts of each egg together. Encourage your child to sort the eggs by colour. If you like, colour the compartments of an egg carton to match the eggs; have your child place each egg in a compartment of the same colour. Store the eggs in the egg carton when not in use.

Memory

This is a great way to recycle wrapping paper. You can also make this a seasonal activity by using wrapping paper in holiday patterns or cutting the cards into shapes such as winter mittens, hearts, or Easter eggs.

> *Wrapping paper in a variety of patterns and colours*
> *3-inch by 5-inch index cards*
> *Glue*
> *Scissors*
> *Clear contact paper*
> *Clothes pegs (optional)*

Cut wrapping paper into 3-inch by 5-inch rectangles, making two rectangles from each pattern or colour of paper. Glue each rectangle to a small index card. Cover both sides of the index card with clear contact paper and trim the edges. Make five to ten pairs of cards (more for older children).

Very young children will enjoy simply handling and looking at the cards. Gradually encourage them to lay the cards out face up and try to clip the matching pairs together with clothes pegs. Older toddlers and preschoolers will enjoy playing a game of Memory, where all cards are laid out face down and each player takes a turn trying to turn over a matching pair.

Store the cards in a Ziploc bag. If you use clothes pegs with this game, store both clothes pegs and cards in a shoebox when not in use.

Postman

Paper card
Scissors
Shoeboxes or plastic baskets
Clear contact paper

Cut circles, squares and triangles out of various colours of paper card. Cover the shapes with clear contact paper. Tape one of each shape (if sorting by shapes) or each colour (if sorting by colours) to a shoebox or small plastic basket. Give the remaining shapes to your child and have her play postman – delivering all the shapes or colours to their proper postboxes. You can also play this game with Lego, wooden blocks, or other items you may have around the house. Try varying the criteria, sorting by big and small, hard and soft and so on. If using baskets, they will stack nicely in a cupboard or on a shelf when not in use. Store the cards in a Ziploc bag with the baskets.

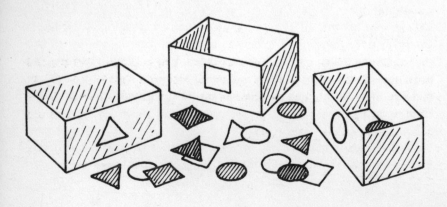

Apple Seed Count

Apple
Knife
Paint (optional)
Paper (optional)

Cut an apple in half and remove all the apple seeds. Count the seeds with your child. Eat the apple for a snack or dip it in paint and onto paper to make an apple print.

Colour Game

Help your child learn her colours and sharpen her listening skills at the same time.

Objects of various colours

Give your child various directions by colour (for example, 'Put the red bear on the table,' 'Pick up the blue car', and 'Bring me the yellow book'). You can also do this with actions based on the colour of your child's clothes: 'If you are wearing green, you may sit down', or 'If you are wearing orange, clap your hands'.

Cars and Colours

Toy cars
Paper card

Start with two cars in two different colours, such as red and blue. Have paper card in red and blue, too. Play with the cars for a while, then 'park' each car on the paper card of the same colour. Be sure to talk about the cars and their colours as you play. Play with the cars some more, then see if your child can park each car on the matching paper. Add another colour as each is mastered.

Colour Match

Paper card
Black marker
Crayons

Give your child a crayon that matches the colour of each piece of paper card. (For very young children, start with only two colours.) If you like, use a black marker to write the name of the colour on each sheet of paper card. Hold up one of the pieces of paper and ask her to pick out the crayon of the same colour, or place the papers and crayons on the table and have her match them up that way. Be sure to use the colour names as you do this (for example, 'I have a red piece of paper. Can you find the red crayon that will match my paper?')

Colour Hunt

Help your toddler learn her colours by going on a colour hunt together.

Paper or plastic bags

Hunting hats (optional)

Begin your colour hunt by putting on your hunting hats and picking a colour to hunt. To begin, show your child an object that represents the colour you're looking for, name the colour, then put it in the bag. Do this two or three times, then let your child be the hunter.

When you are finished, empty your bags and name the items together (red sock, red ball, red cup). You can also hunt for colours (without collecting objects) at the supermarket or when you're driving along together.

Object Matchup

Paper Household objects
Pencil, pen, or marker
Clear contact paper
Scissors
Box or bag

Gather several common household objects, such as a spoon, biscuit cutter, or key (something with a recognisable shape). Place each object on a separate piece of paper and trace around it. Cover the sheets of paper with clear contact paper.

Put all the objects inside a box or bag and spread the pages with the outlined shapes on the table or floor. Have your child remove an object from the box or bag and match it to its outline.

Store the objects and their outlines in a shoebox when not in use.

Search and Sort

Make sure the stones you use for this activity are large enough not to pose a choking hazard.

48 stones (plus a few extras for those that get lost)
4 empty egg cartons
Paint or spray paint in 4 different colours

Paint twelve stones per colour and let dry; if using poster paint, you may want to finish with a clear acrylic spray. If you like, paint each of the egg cartons a different colour.

Give your child the stones and the egg cartons. She will have fun sorting the stones and storing them in the egg cartons. You can also hide the stones in her sandbox for her to dig up and collect in a bucket.

Colourful Clothes Pegs

Craft-type clothes pegs (without springs)
3 empty tins
Paint, crayons, or markers
Paper card or coloured contact paper

Paint or colour 5–6 clothes pegs in the primary colours (red, yellow and blue). Cover each tin with a different primary colour, using paper card or coloured contact paper.

Encourage your older toddler to match the colours as she places the clothes pegs around the rim of the tin.

You can also cut a small hole in the plastic lid of the tin and have her drop the clothes pegs through the lid. Store the clothes pegs in the covered tins when not in use.

Colour Cards

Paper card
Black marker
Scissors
Clear contact paper

Make up two sets of cards from paper card. Start with only a few colours, working your way up to the nine basic colours (red, green, blue, brown, yellow, orange, purple, black and white). If you like, write the names of each colour on the card.

Cover the cards with clear contact paper. Spread the cards out on a table and begin by picking up one of the cards and saying, 'I have a red card. Can you hand me the other red card?'

After a while, your child will enjoy matching the cards all by herself. Store the cards in a small Ziploc bag when not in use.

Paper Plate Numbers

20 small paper plates
Black marker
Stickers or dots

Make up a matching set of paper plates with numbers from one to ten. Put one sticker on the edge of each of two plates and write the numeral 1 and/or the word one in the centre of the plate. Make pairs with the rest of the numerals in the same way. You can use this as a hands-on matching activity or just display the plates on a wall in your child's bedroom or wherever she spends time during the day.

Colour Cube

Empty milk cartons   *Tape*
(any size will do)   *Scissors*
Construction or contact   *Glue*
paper in six different colours *Clear contact paper*

Choose two milk cartons the same size. Measure the base of one carton and mark a cutting line that same distance up the side of the carton. Cut along the line. Cut the other carton in the same way. You should now have two open-ended cubes. Push one cube open-end-down into the other cube. Tape around the cut edges. Cut squares to fit one side of the cube out of six different colours of paper card. Glue one square to each side of the cube. Cover with clear contact paper for durability.

You can use your colour cube in many different ways:

- Have your child throw the cube up in the air; when it lands, ask her to bring you something that matches the colour on top of the cube.
- Cut squares of paper card in the same colours as the cube and cover with clear contact paper. When she tosses the cube in the air, have her hand you the colour card that matches the colour on top of the cube.
- Match the colours on the cube to crayons, toys, or Lego.
- Come up with matching activities of your own. You can also make a shape cube and matching cards and play in the same way.

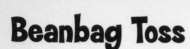

Beanbag Toss

Large sheet of paper
Markers or paints
Beanbag

On a large sheet of paper, draw or paint several large shapes in different colours (or cut shapes out of paper card and lay them on the floor). Have your child stand a few feet away and toss a beanbag onto the shapes. Have her identify the colour and/or shape the beanbag landed on. As she becomes more skilled, ask her to aim for a certain shape (for example, 'Let's try for the red square this time. Oops! You hit the yellow circle!').

Alphabet Sand

Sand, salt, or sugar
Metal pie plate

Pour sand, salt, or sugar into a metal pie plate. Your child can learn her letters by making their shapes with her index finger in the sand. Start with simple letters like O, C, V, or X. Avoid salt if your child has a cut on her finger; avoid sugar if you think she may eat more than she spells!

Tape Shapes

Masking tape or colourful tape

Use masking tape or colourful tape to make several different shapes on the floor. Call out different movements, such as 'Crawl to the square', 'Hop to the circle', or 'Run to the triangle'.

If you like, make a Shape Cube (see Colour Cube, page 179) with the same shapes on it as you have taped on the floor. Throw the Shape Cube into the air and when it lands, have your child move to the same shape as is displayed on the top of the cube.

Practical Maths

Give your child the opportunity to develop maths skills in her everyday world. Count everything with your child: steps as you climb them, toys as you pick them up, cups as you set the table. Take your child on household counting assignments. You can count the number of doors in your house (including closets). Count out loud with your child as you match napkins to place mats, forks to spoons and so on.

Find the Oddball

Sheet of paper, cut in half lengthwise
Markers, shapes cut out of paper card, or stickers
Clear contact paper
Scissors

On each strip of paper make a set of pictures or symbols that are all the same except for one (for example, five happy faces, one sad face; five cat stickers, one dog sticker; five triangles, one circle; and so on). Cover with clear contact paper. Ask your child to find the oddball. Older children can explain how it differs from the others in the set. Store the strips in a large Ziploc bag when not in use.

Sock Matchup

This will help your child match up her socks and learn her numbers at the same time.

Permanent laundry marker
Socks

Number each pair of your child's socks with a permanent laundry marker. You can have her match up her socks as you fold the laundry, or place them in her drawer and have her match them as she wears them.

Shape Matchup

Paper card in 4 different colours
Scissors
Clear contact paper

Cut out two sets of the four basic geometric shapes (circle, triangle, square, rectangle) from paper card, using a different colour for each shape. Cover with clear contact paper. Give one set to your child. Hold up one shape from your set and ask her if she can find the matching shape from her set, being sure to call the shape by its name as you do. ('I have a circle. Can you find a circle, too?')

You can also mix up both sets on the table and have your child pick out the matching shapes. If you think your child is matching by colour or by associating a certain shape with a certain colour, try it again with a new set of shapes in different colours, or make the shapes all the same colour. Store the shapes in a Ziploc bag when not in use.

Number Cube

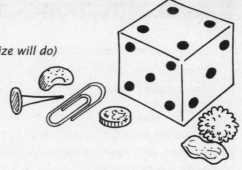

Empty milk cartons (any size will do)
Tape
Paper card
Clear contact paper
Scissors
Permanent marker

Choose two milk cartons the same size. Measure the base of one carton and mark a cutting line that same distance up the side of the carton. Cut along the line. Cut the other carton in the same way. You should now have two ope-ended cubes. Push one cube open-end-down into the other cube. Tape around the cut edges. Wrap the entire cube in a sheet of paper. On each face of the cube use a permanent marker to make a different number of dots (or use dot stickers) from one to six. Cover the cube in clear contact paper.

Give your child six small objects to count with. Show her how to throw the die in the air and count out the same number of objects as dots on the top of the cube. If you like, substitute raisins, small pieces of cereal, or chocolate chips for the objects to count with. Count out the correct number, then eat them!

Playdough Numbers

Paper card or white or coloured paper
Broad-tip marker
Clear contact paper
Playdough

Use a broad-tip marker to write the numerals 0 to 10, using one piece of paper for each numeral. Cover each piece of paper with clear contact paper. Show your child how to roll playdough into ropes and shape the playdough on each piece of paper to match the shape of the numeral.

CHAPTER 9
Music and Movement

'The commonest fallacy among women is that simply having children makes one a mother-which is as absurd as believing that having a piano makes one a musician.'

– Sydney J. Harris

Anyone who has ever watched a baby's reaction to music knows that babies seem to be born with a sense of music and rhythm. Even before they're old enough to walk, many will bob their heads and wiggle their little bodies when lively music comes on. Once they can walk, just try to stop them from jiggling and dancing anytime, anywhere they hear a snappy beat.

Often the first music your child hears will come from you. Don't worry if you can't carry a tune; your voice is the most beautiful one he hears. Sing as you rock him, walk him, carry him, change him, bathe him and play with him. If you don't know many songs, borrow a few tapes or CDs of children's songs from the library, or buy them for your own collection.

Children also seem to have a natural instinct for movement. Once a child can walk, run, jump and climb, there are many days when it seems that is all he wants to do. Movement activities are important because they help your child develop his gross motor skills. Moving to music is equally important, because it helps your child experience movement as it relates to music and rhythm.

Listening to, moving to and making music should be part of every day for you and your child. These activities have many benefits, but for most children they are just plain fun!

Button Tap

Large buttons with 2 holes
Rubber bands
Empty cooking pots
Small gloves (optional)

Insert the looped ends of a rubber band into the two holes of a large button. Bring the looped ends together and slide onto your child's finger. Put a few of these on each hand and let your child tap out some music on an upside-down pot.

For a variation, sew small buttons onto the fingers of a small glove. Place the glove on your child's hand and let him tap around the house.

Strumming Fun

Corrugated cardboard
Spoon

Show your child how to strum a spoon across the ridges on a piece of corrugated cardboard for a neat sound.

Paper Bag Shaker

Paper bag
Rice or dried beans
Ribbon or rubber band

Make a simple shaker for your toddler by putting a small amount of rice or dried beans into a paper bag (you may want to decorate the bag with markers or stickers first). Tie the bag securely with a piece of ribbon or a rubber band. This simple shaker can add a lot of enjoyment to your songs and dance.

Tin Drum

Empty tin with 2 plastic lids
Contact paper or your child's artwork
Glue
Pencil
Empty thread spool

You can create a drum for your child by cutting the bottom out of a tin and covering the can with contact paper (or letting your child draw a picture on some paper and gluing it around the can). Glue plastic lids on each end of the can. Create a drumstick by gluing the lead end of a pencil into the hole of an empty thread spool.

For a variation, an empty paper towel roll and an empty cereal box will make a soft but authentic drum for your toddler.

Toddler Triangle

You may want to cover the sharp ends of the nails with tape before using them.

> *2 large (5-inch) nails*
> *String*

Tie a string around the head of one of the large nails. While holding onto the string, tap the 'triangle' with the other nail.

Tiny Tambourine

> *2 small aluminium tart pans (about 3 inches in diameter)*
> *Dried beans, corn, coins and so on*
> *Stapler or tape*

Put a handful of dried beans, corn, or coins in a small aluminium tart pan. Place another tart pan over the top of the first and staple or tape the edges together.

Easter Egg Maracas

Small plastic Easter eggs
Coins, dried beans, small rocks, popcorn kernels,
beads, buttons and so on
Glue gun
Empty egg carton

Gather a variety of items to fill the plastic Easter eggs. Try coins, dried beans, small rocks, popcorn kernels, beads, buttons and so on. Fill each egg with a different substance and securely glue the two pieces of the egg together. Store in an egg carton. Toddlers will enjoy taking the eggs in and out of the carton and shaking them to hear the different sounds they make.

For an older child, fill two eggs with each substance. Have him shake the eggs and match up the pairs by listening to the sounds they make.

Simple Shaker

Empty film canisters or small plastic bottles
Small rocks, beads, buttons or popcorn kernels

Place a few rocks, beads, buttons, popcorn kernels, or other small objects into an empty film canister or other small plastic container. Glue the lid on securely to prevent a possible choking hazard.

Kazoo

Empty toilet paper roll
Thin paper (newspaper works well)
White glue
Hole punch
Scissors

Punch a hole in the side of the empty toilet paper roll as far from the end as the punch will reach. Cut a square of paper large enough to cover one end of the roll. Coat the edge of the roll with glue and press it firmly onto the square of paper. Leave the roll standing on the paper until the glue is completely dry. If you like, your child can decorate his kazoo with crayons, markers, or stickers.

To play the kazoo, show your child how to put his mouth against the open end of the kazoo and hum.

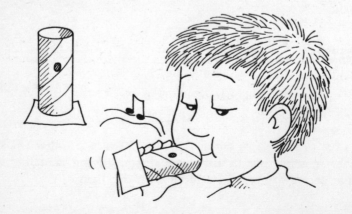

Jingle Bell Roller

Empty tin with lid
Jingle bells or jar lids

Put bells or metal jar lids inside the empty tin. Securely glue or tape the plastic lid onto the tin. Your child can help you decorate the outside of the tin. If you like, try gluing a piece of contact paper sticky side out around the can, then have your toddler stick on pictures cut from magazines, pieces of wrapping paper, or whatever you have on hand. Cover with another piece of contact paper. Your child will have fun shaking the can or rolling it across the floor.

Dance and Fall Down

Music

Put on some music and dance around the room with your child. When the music stops, everyone falls down. When the music begins again, everyone gets up and dances some more.

Dancing with Scarves

Scarves are a versatile item to have on hand for toddlers.

Scarf (chiffon or other lightweight fabric)
Music

Choose a light, breezy scarf for your child to dance with. If the scarf is too long, tie a knot in the middle to form a handle. Encourage your child to wave his scarf in the air in time to the music.

Stop!

Face your child and hold his hands. Walk slowly in a circle and sing or recite this poem as you walk:

Round and round and round we go,
Round and round and round we go,
Round and round and round we go.
Round and round and STOP!

Freeze when you say 'STOP!' Repeat the game as many times as your child wants to, changing directions and speeding up a little more each time.

Follow the Leader

Young children are such a bundle of energy. A short 'exercise class' not only helps their large muscle development, but it can also be a sanity saver on a long, rainy day indoors. You'll feel better afterward, too!

Encourage your child to follow your lead as you exercise together. Try touching toes, running in place, swinging your arms and stretching to the ceiling. Exercise to music, pass a ball back and forth, or twirl a long ribbon in the air. For a change, let your child be the leader and you follow his example.

Let's Pretend

This activity will give your child's large muscles a workout along with his imagination.

Give your child a series of instructions such as 'Let's pretend you are a rabbit. Can you hop like a rabbit?' or 'Let's pretend you are an elephant. Can you walk about like a big, heavy elephant?' Try other animals and include things such as plants growing in the ground, a flower opening on a summer day, or a balloon being filled with air.

Jingle Bell Bracelet

You might consider this most appropriate as a Christmas activity, but toddlers will enjoy jingling any time of year.

Jingle bells
Elastic cord
Scissors

Cut the elastic cord long enough to fit your child's wrist and add a few inches for tying. String three or four jingle bells onto the elastic and tie the ends together. Slip the bracelet onto your child's wrist or ankle, put some music on and listen to the bells jingle as he dances or claps around the house.

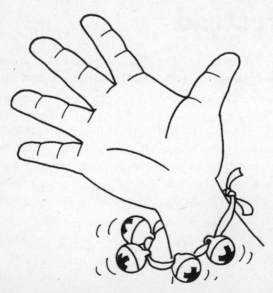

Climbing Practise

Couch cushions or large pillows

Make a big, soft pile of sofa cushions or large pillows on the floor. Your toddler will have fun climbing and rolling around on them. For older toddlers, stack the cushions up like stairs against the sofa and let him practice climbing up and down.

Toddler Trampoline

Cot mattress
Cot sheet
Pillows

Place a cot mattress on the floor, away from any dangerous edges or corners. Cover the mattress with a cot sheet and surround it with pillows for safety. Your child will enjoy jumping and bouncing on his toddler-sized trampoline.

Mirror Play

This activity will probably be best enjoyed by one-year-olds.

Large mirror

Stand or sit with your child in front of a large mirror. Ask your child what he sees and point out his head, arms, legs, feet and so on. Encourage him to make movements and watch what happens to his reflection as he does. Put on some music and watch him move and dance in time to the beat. You may want to have your camera on hand in case he tries to kiss his reflection.

Toddler Gymnastics

Simple gymnastics will not only burn up some of your toddler's seemingly endless energy, but it will also encourage his eye/hand coordination, necessary for balance and depth perception.

Encourage your toddler in simple gymnastics such as tumbling, rolling, climbing and sliding. If you like, put on some snappy music or play Follow the Leader. Show your child the basic movements, then take turns being the leader.

Dance Ribbon

Empty key chain or plastic shower curtain ring
Long lengths of brightly coloured ribbon or plastic

Attach 3- or 4-foot lengths of brightly coloured ribbon or plastic to an empty key chain or plastic shower curtain ring. Your child can wave the ribbon in the air as he runs or twirl it in time to the music as he dances.

CHAPTER 10
Arts and Crafts

'It would seem that something which means poverty, disorder and violence every single day should be avoided entirely, but the desire to beget children is a natural urge.'

– Phyllis Diller

Art and craft activities provide many valuable learning experiences for toddlers. Your child will begin to learn to think creatively and activities such as drawing, painting, cutting, pasting and playing with playdough and other craft materials will help develop fine motor and manipulative skills.

One important thing to keep in mind when doing any art or craft activity with a young child is that it's the process – not the product – that counts. By this I mean that activities which can provide so much benefit to a toddler can also lead to frustration and disappointment for both adult and child if the parent or care-giver comes to the activity with a final product in mind. The adult who has an expected outcome from a toddler art or craft activity will, out of necessity, do a lot of the work for the child. The child will end up with a nice picture or object, but any skills she may have learned from that experience will be lost or minimised.

Even something as simple as using a glue stick is important for little ones, so resist the urge to grab it out of your child's hands and do it yourself if she's not doing it 'right'. We all know arts and crafts look better, go faster and are neater if we do the work for our children, but if they're to gain any benefit at all from an activity, they have to do the work themselves.

Karen Miller, in her book *More Things to Do with Toddlers and Twos* (Telshare Publishing, 1990), lists five general principles for doing art with toddlers. While she is writing primarily for teachers of toddlers, these are great guidelines to keep in mind whether you're working with many toddlers or just one.

1. Don't tell your child what to make and don't expect her final product to be recognisable. Telling a two-year-old to make a postbox or an Easter basket only sets her up for failure, as she cannot possibly do it herself. Instead, Miller says, 'value the basic scribble'. The most important thing for your child is the experience of freely exploring art and craft materials. Toddlers simply cannot control the materials well enough to make a representational drawing.

2. Focus on providing interesting materials. Toddlers are basically interested in cause and effect, whether they are playing with water, building with blocks, or working on an art project such as finger-painting, pasting, or painting with a brush. Your goal in providing your toddler with art experiences should be to expose her to as many different materials and processes as possible. Let her play with warm playdough one day, cold the next; mix paint thick one time, thin another; use wide and narrow paintbrushes as well as sponges, cotton swabs and feathers for painting.

3. Let your child do the whole project. The activity only has value for the child if she does it herself. In making a collage with glue, the value for the child comes in spreading the glue on the page, noticing how it feels on her fingers and so on. If you spread the glue on and

then provide the items for your child to stick to the page, much of the value of the activity is lost.

4. Do art with one child at a time or with very small groups. Miller says that 'with your undivided attention, the child can really concentrate on the material in front of her and enjoy seeing what she can do with it'. If you do have other young children to care for, have other interesting things prepared for them to do while you're working one-on-one with your toddler, or allow them to stand around and watch if they want to. Older two-and three-year-olds may enjoy doing art in groups of three or four.

5. Allow children to repeat experiences. Sometimes we may feel that providing our children with a variety of experiences means never doing the same thing twice. What we're really doing, however, is not allowing our child to fully explore an activity, meaning that the child cannot learn or develop as much. Allowing your toddler to repeat an activity several times gives her the opportunity to fully explore it and, as Miller states, 'encourages the development of concentration and experimentation, both elements of creativity'.

Don't forget to display the artwork your child has created. Post it on walls, doors and of course the refrigerator. Use it to create a custom tablecloth: cover your table with a plain dark tablecloth, arrange your child's artwork on it, then cover with a clear vinyl tablecloth. Use your child's artwork as a gift or wrapping paper when possible. If you like, create a portfolio for your child. Use a three-ring binder and plastic page protectors to save some of your child's earliest or most outstanding creations. (Be sure to date or write your child's age on each work of art.) For extra-large or three-dimensional projects, take a photo or two and put those in the binder.

The activities in this chapter will help you provide your toddler with a variety of art and craft experiences. These experiences should be fun for you and your child, so don't undertake painting or other messy projects when you're tired, rushed, or otherwise unable to devote yourself fully to what your toddler is doing. With the right attitude, you and your toddler will have a wonderful time creating, exploring and discovering the world of art.

Scribbling and Drawing

When I first became a mother, I purchased a very good book on things to do with babies. It stated that children should start to scribble between nine and twelve months of age and it even outlined the procedure to follow: seat your child comfortably, then give her some paper and a big fat crayon. Show her how to make marks on the page, then watch her go.

I was horrified to realise that time had gotten away from me! My daughter, already past her first birthday, had not yet had her first experience with crayons and paper. After a quick run to the shop, I optimistically seated her in her highchair, taped down a piece of blank paper, showed her how to hold the crayon and let her go to it. You can imagine my dismay when she began eating the crayon and tearing the paper! She wasn't lagging behind developmentally, as I initially feared; she just wasn't ready for the whole scribbling experience.

When ready for it, most toddlers will find scribbling a lot of fun. It allows them to experiment with cause and effect while developing small muscles and hand/eye coordination. Cynthia Catlin, in her book *Toddlers Together: The Complete Planning Guide for a Toddler Curriculum* (Gryphon House, 1994), says:

Scribbling is the precursor to writing, just as babbling is to talking. A better term for scribbling would be M.I.M.s, for these are the Most Important Marks a toddler can make.

Provide your toddler with a variety of drawing tools and materials: crayons, markers, pens, pencil crayons and chalk. For drawing paper, use paper card, newsprint, fine sandpaper, or cut-open grocery bags. Remember to include three-dimensional surfaces such as boxes and rocks.

If replacing caps on markers is a problem, make this simple marker holder: mix plaster of Paris in a small plastic container that is at least as deep as a marker top. Set the marker tops in the wet plaster with the open end up. Be sure that the plaster does not cover the open end of the marker top. When the plaster dries, press the markers into their tops that have dried into the plaster. Remind your child to stand the markers back in the marker holder when she has finished using them.

Rainbow Crayons

This idea appears in *The Preschooler's Busy Book*, but it's worth repeating here. These crayons are beautiful and easy for little hands to hold!

Broken crayon pieces
Clean, empty tin cans
Pot of hot water
Empty plastic film canisters

This is a great way to use broken crayons. Remove any paper from the crayons and sort them by colour. Place the pieces, one colour at a time, in the empty tin cans. Set the tin cans in a pot of very hot or boiling water until the crayons have melted. Pour a small amount (approximately a quarter inch) into each film canister. When the wax hardens, add a second colour in the same way. When you're done, you will have a crayon rainbow of layered colours.

Cylinder Pictures

Paper
Markers or crayons
Tape

Have your child draw on a rectangular piece of paper. When she's done, roll the paper into a cylinder and tape the ends together. Set it on a shelf or mantle for all to admire.

Marker Drawing

Here's a good way to get more use out of dried-up markers.

Dried-up markers
Water
Paper

Let your child dip dried-up markers in water and use them like water-colours on paper. When the tips turn white, you can throw the markers away or dip them in paint and use them as paintbrushes.

Foot Tracing

Drawing paper
Crayons, markers or paints

Have your child stand on a piece of paper while you trace around her feet with a pen or crayon. Then trace your own feet and compare sizes. Colour the feet with crayons, markers, or paints. Older children may want to use crayons, markers, or paint to add nail polish and funny rings to the toes.

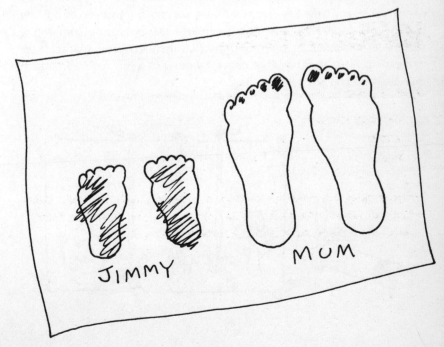

Toddler Mural

Toddlers love to colour and will usually colour on anything and everything if you let them.

Tape a large sheet of drawing paper to an easel. Cut several pieces of wool about 2 feet in length. Cut a small notch at one end of each crayon and wrap and tie a length of wool around it. Tie the other end of the wool to the top of the easel. (Be sure to cut the wool long enough to reach the paper, but not so long that it poses a choking hazard.) Now your toddler can scribble any time she wants without waiting for you to set out the crayons and paper. If you don't have an art easel but do have an empty wall in the basement or playroom, use that instead. Tape a large sheet of paper to the wall. Above the paper, hammer in a few nails and attach the wool and crayons to the nails.

Chalk Fun

There was a time that chalk was just for chalk-boards and pavements. Now inexpensive chalk is available in a variety of colours and thicknesses and you can use it creatively in many different art endeavours. The following ideas will help you use chalk in ways you may not have considered before.

Chalk
Paper
Hair spray (optional)
Water (optional)
Sponge (optional)
Liquid starch and/or buttermilk (optional)
Paintbrush (optional)
Sugar (optional)
Cotton balls (optional)

- Draw with chalk on a piece of plain paper or paper card. Spray with hair spray to set the chalk.
- Wet your paper with a damp sponge and draw on the wet paper with chalk.
- Paint a piece of paper with liquid starch. While it's still wet, make designs with coloured chalk.
- Brush buttermilk over the surface of your paper, then use chalk to draw on it.
- Place a piece of paper on a textured surface (such as a pavement) or over a greeting card with a raised design. Rub a piece of chalk sideways over the paper to make a chalk rubbing of the texture or design.

- Draw on a window with wet chalk. It will easily wash away when you're done.
- Soak chalk in a mixture of 1 cup water and ⅓ cup sugar for 5 to 10 minutes. Draw with the wet chalk on a piece of paper. Use a cotton ball to smudge the chalk marks on the paper.

Painting

A child's love for paint begins at an early age and lasts for many years, if not a lifetime. A clean sheet of paper before her, pots of paint in vivid colours, big paintbrushes to wield as she wills–what could make a toddler happier?

If proper preparations have been made, this art experience can be enjoyed by the parent or care-giver, too. Before you begin a painting session with your toddler, consider the following guidelines:

- Don't undertake a painting session with your toddler when you're tired, rushed or otherwise unable to devote yourself fully to what your child is doing.
- Cover up the work space appropriately. I cover the kitchen table with a big old sheet that I throw in the wash when the painting session is over.
- If you don't have a painter's smock or big old T-shirt to cover your child, dress her in old clothes that you can afford to set aside as painting clothes. (Even washable paints may not wash out completely.)
- Add a little washing-up liquid or water and soap flakes to the paint. It makes cleaning-up easier.

The best kind of paint for young children is poster paint, which you can buy at any art store in pre-mixed liquid form or as a powder that must be mixed with water. You can also make your own poster paint using the recipes in Appendix A. Children rarely need more than three colours: red, blue and yellow.

Teach your child how to mix these colours to create others. Poster paint blocks are also available. They're practical because they don't have to be diluted and they can't be spilled, making cleanup easier. In addition, paint blocks are economical and last a long time.

However, your child will probably not find them as fun as slick liquid paints. Empty baby-food jars work well as paint jars. You can use a sponge to prevent the jar from tipping and soak up any drips. Simply cut a hole in the sponge the size of the jar and fit the jar into the sponge. You can also make a simple toddler-size paint palette by gluing plastic milk lids to a piece of heavy cardboard. Pour a small amount of paint into each lid. For a more permanent palette, nail several babyfood jar lids to a block of wood.

Paper can be purchased from an art supply shop, but consider some of the following alternatives. Newsprint is a wonderful paper for painting and roll ends can be purchased cheaply from a newspaper publisher. Visit your local printer and ask if you can leave an empty box for a week or two. She may agree to fill it with all kinds of wonderful paper that would otherwise be discarded. Also try fine sandpaper as an alternative art paper for a wonderful effect. For finger-painting, use the shiny side of freezer paper that can be purchased at the supermarket. It's much cheaper than special finger-paint paper and works just as well.

✂ Arts and Crafts ────────────────

If you have an old wall you don't care too much about, cover it with a large piece of contact paper. You can tape the painting paper directly to the contact paper and it will wipe up easily. The contact paper will likely damage the wall if you try to remove it, so be careful where you put it.

A tabletop easel can be made by removing one side of a cardboard box and taping the remaining three sides to form a triangle shape. Tape one side to the table and attach a piece of paper to one of the other sides. Use it for painting or drawing. Here are a few more tips to keep in mind when working with paint:

- Water and soap flakes or detergent added to paint make it easier to wash out.
- Liquid detergent added to paint will help prevent cracking.
- Liquid starch will make paint thicker.
- Condensed milk will give paint a glossier finish.
- Powdered alum can be used as a preservative.
- Salt, crushed eggshells and coffee grounds give paint an interesting texture.
- Baby powder mixed with poster paint will extend the paint and add a nice smell.
- Plastic cafeteria trays are ideal for toddlers to paint on, with or without paper.
- String up a line in the playroom or kitchen that can be used to hang paintings to dry. Wet artwork can be attached to the line with clothes pegs. When dry, be sure to display your child's paintings prominently. Think of creative uses for some of her work: Many painting projects make wonderful wrapping or greeting cards.

Straw Painting

If your child has mastered the skill of blowing, she may enjoy this activity. If not, she will still enjoy using the straw as a paintbrush.

Poster paint
Paper
Drinking straw

Drop a bit of thin paint on a piece of paper. Give your child a straw and have her blow the paint around. If you like, add a second and third colour. You can also try different types of paper for different effects.

Paint with Water

Black marker
Paper towel
Paintbrush
Water

Draw a picture or shape with a thick black marker on a piece of paper towel. Show your child how to brush water over the marker lines and watch how the colours seep out.

Dry Painting

For a painting activity, this is pretty clean and requires little preparation.

Cotton balls
Clothes pegs (spring-type)
Powdered poster paint
Paper
Hair spray

Clip a cotton ball onto the end of a springtype peg. Sprinkle a few colours of powdered poster paint onto a piece of paper. Show your toddler how to use the cotton ball to spread the paint around the paper. When the painting is done, spray it with hair spray to set the paint. It will make a nice greeting card.

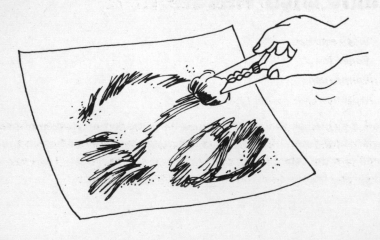

Crumple Painting

Here's another easy way for your young child to make wrapping paper.

Liquid poster paint or soap paint
(see Frosty Soap Painting, page 226)
Newspaper
Heavy plain paper

Crumple up some newspaper into a ball and dip it in liquid poster or soap paint. Press the newspaper ball lightly all over the heavy plain paper. Use two or three different colours if you like. Let dry.

Food Colouring Painting

Food colouring
Water
Paintbrush
Paper towel or coffee filter

Add food colouring to water, enough to achieve the colour you want. Brush the food colouring and water mixture onto a piece of paper towel or coffee filter. Use several colours. When the paper towel is soaked, remove and let dry, then mount on paper card to display.

Sheet Painting

Spray bottle
Water
Liquid poster paint
Old sheet

Fill a spray bottle half with water and half with poster paint. For some creative outdoor fun, hang an old sheet on a fence or clothesline and have your child spraypaint it.

Paint Lollies

Please supervise this activity carefully and use it only with children who are not likely to lick these lollies. For safer variations for really young children, try Ice lolly Painting or Ice Cube Painting.

Liquid poster paint
Water
Lolly mould
Paper

Mix one part poster paint with one part water and pour into a lolly mould. Insert sticks and place in the freezer until frozen.

Remove paint lollies from the freezer about 10 minutes before you want to use them. Give your child the paint lolly and a large piece of paper and let her paint away.

Fly Swatter Painting

This is definitely an outdoor activity. If it's just 'something to do,' then one colour of paint is enough. For a nicer-looking painting, try using two or three colours of paint, one after the other.

Fly swatter
Paint
Baking pan or biscuit sheet
Large sheets of paper

Put up large sheets of paper outside, either by taping them to a fence or clipping them to a clothesline. Pour paint into the baking tray. Show your child how to dip the fly swatter into the paint and slap it onto the paper.

Rainbow Painting

Paper
Water
Wide paintbrush or sponge
Paints or washable markers

Paint a sheet of paper with water using a wide paintbrush or a wet sponge. Your child can paint lines of colour across the page with paints, or draw on it with washable markers. The wet paper really makes the colours flow and blend for a beautiful effect.

Ice Lolly Painting

This variation of Paint Lollies is more suited to younger children. If you think your child may lick the ice lolly after it's been used to paint, try substituting jelly powder for powdered paint.

Water
Lolly mould
Powdered poster paint
Paper

Freeze water in a lolly mould to make ice lollies. Remove from the freezer a few minutes before using to allow the ice to melt a little. Sprinkle a little poster paint powder on a piece of paper. Your child can paint by rubbing the ice lolly over the paint on the paper.

Bathtub Finger-painting

Finger-paint
Newsprint

This is a great idea for the youngest artists in your house. Dress your one-year-old in a nappy and an old shirt. Place her in a dry bathtub with a blob of finger-paint and watch the results! When her work is complete, lay a piece of newsprint over it, press gently and lift for a copy of her masterpiece.

Ice Cube Painting

Ice cubes
Paper
Powdered poster paint
Flat box or large baking tray

Place a sheet of paper in the box or baking tray. Sprinkle a little poster paint powder on the paper. Place the ice cube in the box and let your child rotate the box around to make a pretty painting.

Squeeze Painting

Flour, Salt
Water
Food colouring or liquid poster paint (optional)
Squeeze bottles or small spoons
Paper

Mix equal parts of flour, salt and water together. If working on coloured paper, leave the paint white; if using white paper, add a few drops of food colouring or liquid poster paint to the paint. Pour the paint into squeeze bottles or use a small spoon to dribble the paint onto the paper. Let dry and admire the sparkly results.

Cling Film Painting

White paper
Paint
Spoons
Plastic cling film

Using a spoon, dribble paint onto the paper. Use several different colours. Place a sheet of plastic cling film over the paint (make sure the cling film covers the whole surface). Use your hands to smooth the cling film over the paper, then carefully peel it off. Allow the painting to dry.

Painted Place Mat

Rubber cement
White paper card
Poster paint
Paintbrushes
Clear contact paper

Dribble rubber cement randomly or in a design over a sheet of white paper card. Allow to dry for about 30 minutes, then paint over the rubber cement using poster paint in one or more colours. Allow the paint to dry, then peel the rubber cement off the paper card to see the design that is left. Cover both sides of the painting with clear contact paper to make it into a place mat.

Feather Painting

For this activity you can use colourful feathers from the craft store or bird feathers you find outside.

Feathers
Glue
Poster paint
Paper

Mix a little bit of glue with the poster paint. Use feathers to brush the paint onto the paper. If you like, leave a few feathers on the painting to make a feather collage. (When the paint dries, the glue mixed with it will make the feathers stick.) You can also try this with pine branches, leaves, flowers, or other natural objects that may be good for painting.

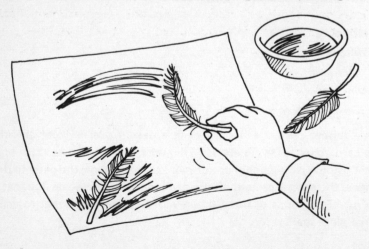

Rock Painting

Golf balls or ping-pong balls also work well for this activity.

Shoebox with lid
Paper
Scissors
Poster paint
Rock

Cut a piece of plain paper or paper card to fit the bottom of the shoebox. Pour a small amount of paint into a dish and dip a rock in the paint. Place the rock into the shoebox or container and shut the lid.

Shake the box up and down and from side to side. Open the lid and look at the design the rock has made. Dip the rock in another colour of paint and repeat the shaking procedure until your child tires of it.

Paint Dancing

Large sheet or piece of fabric
Baking tray for paint
Liquid poster paint
Warm, soapy water
Towels
Music

Tape a large sheet or piece of fabric securely to the floor or lay it on the ground outside. Fill a baking tray with paint. Add a little liquid soap or washing-up liquid to make cleaning-up easier.

Put on some music and roll up your child's trouser legs, or dress her in only a nappy or shorts. Have her step into the tray of paint, then onto the bedsheet.

Then have her dance to the music! Have a pan of warm, soapy water and a towel on hand for when she tires of this activity (or if she refuses to stay on the sheet).

Paint Pen

This idea from *The Preschooler's Busy Book* is such a great activity for toddlers that I thought it worth repeating.

> *Empty roll-on deodorant bottle or shoe polish bottle*
> *Liquid poster paint*

To make a giant paint pen for your child, pry the top off a rollon deodorant or shoe polish bottle. Fill it with poster paint (mixed fairly thickly) and snap the top back on the bottle. Your child can use this for a quick and easy painting activity.

Frosty Soap Painting

> *1 cup washing powder*
> *½ cup cold water*
> *Electric mixer or wire whisk*
> *Food colouring (optional)*
> *Paintbrushes*
> *Heavy paper or cardboard*

Beat or whisk cold water and washing powder together until stiff. Add food colouring or leave white if using coloured paper. Paint with a brush or use as fingerpaint on heavy paper or cardboard. Let dry flat.

String Painting

Wool or string
Scissors
Tape
Lolly sticks
Liquid poster paint
Paper

Tape 5-inch pieces of wool or string to the end of a lolly stick. Using the stick as a handle, dip the string into liquid poster paint and drag it across and around the paper.

Finger-painting

Finger-paints
Finger-paint paper

Finger-painting is a wonderfully messy adventure that every child should experience after the age of two – or younger, if you can stand it! Unfortunately, it can be frustrating for parents, as the amount of work required to set up and clean up never seems to merit the 5 minutes (or less) most children will spend at this activity. That said, be prepared for a great big mess and make sure your child wears an art smock.

Wet the paper first to allow the paint to slide better. Drop a blob of paint on the paper and let your child go at it. You can buy commercial finger-paint or make your own using the recipes in Appendix A.

For variety, use finger-paint that has been chilled or warmed. Add salt or sand for texture. Thick finger-paint or finger-paint mixed with salt or sand can also be pushed around the paper with a lolly stick or spoon.

If you like, have your child finger-paint on a table-top or highchair tray, then press a piece of paper over the paint to make a print to save. Plastic cafeteria trays are great surfaces for finger-painting, or try painting on a window or mirror. (Adding a little liquid detergent to the paint makes cleanup easier.)

Print-making

Print-making involves making an impression of an object on paper or another surface. The object to be printed can be covered in paint with a brush or roller, dipped in paint or pressed on a print pad.

A print pad can be made by wadding up newspaper and soaking it in liquid poster paint. Or you can place a thin sponge in a shallow tray or small bowl and cover with several tablespoons of paint. For some print-making, an ink pad can be used. To cushion a print, place a newspaper under the paper on which the impression is to be made.

Many different types of paper can be used for printing: newsprint, paper card and brown paper bags are some of the cheaper options. As with many of the painting projects in this chapter, you can use these printing activities to create some great environmentally friendly wrapping paper.

Very young toddlers are not likely to understand the print-making process. They tend to use the object to be printed more like a sponge or paintbrush and usually end up just pushing it around the paper. Older two and three-year-olds will enjoy making prints. Encourage them to press the object gently into the paint and then onto the paper to make a successful print.

Bubble-Wrap Printing

Bubble-wrap
Tape
Liquid poster paint (several different colours)
Paintbrush
Paper

Tape the bubble wrap to the table or surface you will be painting on. Have your child paint on the bubble wrap, then press a piece of paper on it to get an interesting print.

Cork Printing

Wine bottle corks
Liquid poster paint in a shallow pan
Paper

Grasp the cork at one end and hold it upright. Press the cork into the paint then onto a piece of paper or newsprint. If you like, use poster paint in several different colours.

Block Printing

Small blocks of wood
Zigzag trim
Glue
Liquid poster paint in a shallow pan
Paper

Glue zigzag trim to the end of a block of wood. Press the block into the paint, then onto paper to make a zigzag design. Move the block around in different directions and add different colours of paint if you like.

For an alternate activity, wrap string around a block or glue an object such as a key or small plastic ring to the end of the block to make an interesting print.

Muffin Tin Printing

Muffin tin
Liquid poster paint (several different colours)
Paintbrush
Paper

Place a muffin tin upside down on a covered surface. Have your child paint the bottoms of the muffin cups. When she's done, place a piece of paper over the muffin tin and press to make a print of her work.

Glue Printing

Various objects to print
White glue
Glitter
Paper

Instead of using paint or an ink pad for printing, try using glue and glitter. Press objects (fruits and vegetables cut in half, sponges cut into shapes, string wrapped around a block of wood and so on) into glue, then onto paper. Sprinkle the paper with glitter or coloured sand and let dry. Large pieces of newsprint paper covered with glitter make nice wrapping paper.

Toy Car Printing

Toy cars or trucks with wide wheels
Liquid poster paint
Paper

Pour a small amount of paint in a container big enough to dip the wheels of the toy car or truck in. Place the car or truck into the paint and roll it back and forth a time or two so that the wheels are covered with paint. Roll the car or truck across the paper to make tyre tracks.

Sponge Printing

Sponge
Chalk
Water
Paper

Soak a sponge in water and squeeze to release the excess. Use a piece of chalk to draw on the wet sponge. Press the wet sponge onto a piece of white or coloured paper card to create a print. If you like, use chalk in various colours and a variety of sponges in different shapes and sizes.

Lego Printing

Lego pieces in different sizes
Liquid poster paint
Paper

Pour a small amount of paint into a container big enough to dip the Lego in. Place the Lego upside down in the paint. Press the paint-covered Lego onto the paper to make a print. Use both sides of the Lego and different colours of paint for an interesting design.

Cardboard Printing

Corrugated cardboard
Tape or rubber band
Liquid poster paint
Paper card

Cut a strip of corrugated cardboard about 6 inches by 10 inches. Make sure the corrugated ridges run parallel to the 6-inch sides. Place the cardboard on the table in front of you, smooth side up.

Starting with a 6-inch side, roll up the cardboard tightly. Make sure the corrugated ridges end up on the outside of the roll. Secure the roll with tape or a rubber band. Dip the end of the cardboard roll into the paint and press onto paper to make a flower-like print.

Spool Printing

Print pad or liquid poster paint
Empty thread spools
Paper

Press empty thread spools onto a print pad or dip them in liquid poster paint. Press onto paper to make the shape of a tyre.

Paper Bag Faces

Some toddlers may lose interest in this activity once the paper bag is stuffed. That's okay, because the real value of this activity for the toddler is in the tearing of paper.

Newspaper or old magazines for tearing
Paper bag
Rubber band
Crayon, marker or paint

Tear up old newspapers or magazines. Crumple up the pieces and stuff them in a paper bag. When the bag is full, seal the end with a rubber band. Then draw or paint a big happy face on the paper bag. This item will work well as a large, lightweight object for your toddler to lift, carry, or throw.

Tearing, Gluing and Sticking

Toddlers, paper and glue are a great combination. What child hasn't discovered early in life the special joy of scrunching and tearing paper? Keep a stack of old magazines on hand for tearing. (Most toddlers and young preschoolers can't yet handle a pair of scissors, so avoid frustration and tear everything.)

Gluing is great fun, too. Toddlers enjoy the glue itself as much as whatever it is you're having them make. Vary the type of glue your child uses: a glue stick, glue in a bottle, or spreadable paste. Pour a small amount of white glue into a babyfood jar lid and add a drop or two of food colouring. Use a small paintbrush or cotton swab to spread the glue around.

Provide your child with lots of interesting things to stick: greeting cards, fabric scraps and paper scraps (tissue, wrapping and paper card). You can also use pasta, wool, cotton balls and bits of ribbon. Outdoor walks can yield a wonderful supply of new materials including leaves, pine needles, flower petals and so on. You should also vary the surface onto which your child sticks things: paper plates, cardboard pieces, egg cartons, empty tissue boxes and paper of all shapes, sizes and colours.

The most important thing about tearing, gluing and sticking is that your child should do the whole project by herself. Varying the materials used will keep the same basic activity interesting for both you and your child.

Popcorn Picture

Popped popcorn
Glue stick or white glue
Paper card
Brown paper bag (optional)
Poster paint powder (optional)

Rub the glue stick on a piece of paper card or spread white glue with a brush. Stick popped popcorn onto the paper card to make a collage. For a winter scene, use plain white popcorn. For spring blossoms, shake the popcorn in a brown paper bag with powdered poster paint, then glue the popcorn onto a flower shape cut from paper card. For variety, try using Cheerios or puffed rice cereal instead.

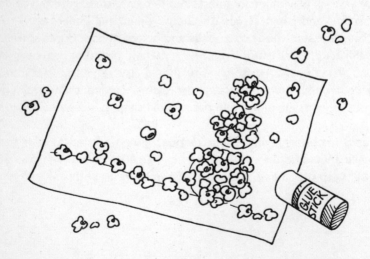

Wrapping Paper Collage

Wrapping paper
Tissue paper
Scissors
Paper card
Glue stick
Clear contact paper (optional)

Save pieces of wrapping paper and tissue paper from birthdays and other occasions. Cut or tear the paper into interesting shapes and save in a box or Ziploc freezer bag.

Show your child how to rub the glue stick onto a piece of paper and then how to press a colourful paper shape onto the glued area. If you like, use a piece of clear contact paper taped to the table sticky side up in place of the paper card and glue.

Tissue Paper Collage

Tin foil
Coloured tissue paper
Scissors (optional)
Baby oil
Paintbrush

Tear off a piece of tin foil about the size of a piece of tissue paper. Cut or tear the tissue paper into small pieces. Squeeze a few drops of baby oil onto the tin foil and spread around with a paintbrush. Show your child how the tissue paper will stick to the foil wherever the baby oil is, but can be easily removed. Use different colours of tissue paper to make a collage.

Salt Pictures

Salt (or clean sand)
Poster paint powder
Empty salt and pepper shakers or spice containers
Paper
Glue
Paintbrush or spoon

Mix salt or sand with poster paint powder in small shakertype containers, one for each colour. Brush glue onto paper with a small brush or dribble it on with a spoon. (Little ones may enjoy smearing the glue around with their fingers.) Sprinkle the salt/paint mixture over the paper. When the glue is dry, tip off the excess salt and hang to display.

Wax Paper Art

A safe and easy alternative to grated crayons and an iron.

Glue
Liquid poster paint or food colouring
Paintbrush
Wax paper
Colourful leaves

Mix glue with poster paint or food colouring to achieve a bright colour (or use coloured glue thinned with a little water). Using a brush, paint glue onto two pieces of wax paper of the same size (the paper should be well coated with glue). Stick colourful leaves onto the glue on one piece of paper, then cover with the other sheet. Press together to stick, then hang in a window.

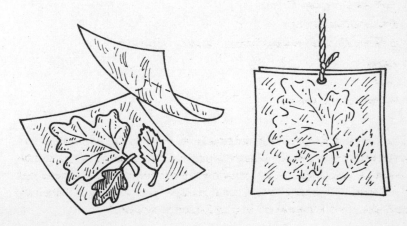

Glitter Shapes

Paper card

Scissors

Glue stick

Glitter or confetti

Small shoebox with lid

Rubber bands

Cut shapes out of paper card. Use basic geometric shapes such as circles, squares, triangles, or rectangles, or seasonal shapes such as hearts, pumpkins, stars and so on. Rub the glue stick on one or both sides of the shapes. Put the glue-covered shape into the shoebox along with confetti or glitter. Place the lid on the shoebox and secure with a couple of rubber bands. Shake the box to cover the shape with glitter or confetti. Remove the shape from the box and allow to dry.

Tape Collage

Toddlers and tape go together in a special way.

Tape (masking, cellophane, coloured and so on)
Small can or plastic container
Paper card

Use an upside-down can (such as a tuna can) or plastic container as a tape holder for your child. Cut or tear off various lengths of tape and place them around the edges of the tape holder so that your child can pull them off easily. Use as many different types and colours of tape as you can. Give your child a piece of paper card and show her how to pull a piece of tape off the tape holder and stick it onto the paper to make a collage.

Spaghetti Mobiles

If your child is likely to eat the glue-covered noodles, substitute golden syrup thinned with a little water for the glue. Many toddlers will enjoy just playing with warm spaghetti on a highchair tray or table top.

White glue (or syrup)
Food colouring in 2–3 different colours
Containers for glue
Cooked spaghetti noodles
Styrofoam meat tray
Wool or ribbon

Decide how many colours of glue you want to make and pour the glue into that many containers. Add a few drops of food colouring to each glue container, using a different colour for each container. Show your child how to dip the spaghetti, one piece at a time, into the coloured glue and lay it on the Styrofoam meat tray. Repeat, using different colours of glue, until your child tires of this activity. Let the noodles dry, then remove from the meat tray, tie on a piece of wool or ribbon and hang from the ceiling as a mobile.

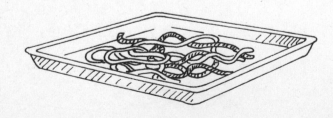

Pathfinding

This is an excellent activity for developing small muscles. Using scissors is too tough for young toddlers, but older two- or three-year-olds can definitely give it a try. If paper is too difficult to cut, try playdough instead.

Pen or pencil
Paper
Child's scissors

Draw an easy-to-cut pattern (using two lines to form a path) on a plain piece of paper. Paths could follow a variety of shapes: zigzags, s-shapes, straight lines and so on. Have your child cut right down the centre of the path without straying. If you like, keep your child's cutting exercises in a special folder that you can add to each day.

Crafts and Other Fun Things to Make

Craft projects will challenge your child's imagination and artistic ability and they will facilitate the development of fine motor skills. They may also fill in the long hours of a rainy day, keeping your child stimulated and happy.

Don't forget that for toddlers, it's the process that counts – not the product. Don't be discouraged if your child won't do it the 'right' way. Perhaps she's still too young to be working on these crafts, or perhaps you need to let her freely explore the craft materials she's using to create a masterpiece of her own.

Toddler Collage

You may do this activity in one sitting or spread it out over a couple of days by adding interesting objects as you find them.

Clear contact paper

Scissors

Variety of objects to stick

Paper card (optional)

Cut two pieces of clear contact paper about the size of a piece of paper, or larger if you like. Remove the backing from one piece of contact paper and lay it on a flat surface such as a table or highchair tray, sticky side up. Tape the corners to the table or highchair tray so that the contact paper won't move around. (If you're planning on working on the collage over a couple of days, tape the contact paper to a cardboard box that can be moved out of the way when you're not working on it.)

Provide a variety of interesting objects for your toddler to stick to the contact paper. Try scraps of tissue or wrapping paper, bits of colourful wool or ribbon, small pieces of pasta, cotton balls, or leaves or flower petals. When her collage is done, cover it with the other piece of contact paper, or use a piece of paper card instead. Hang in a window or on the wall for all to admire, or use as a unique place mat.

Sticker Art

Stickers come in handy for making quick crafts and matching games, decorating cards and gifts, making charts and so on. Children of all ages love stickers. Now is the time to begin a collection, if you haven't started one already.

Stickers
Paper
Paper plate (optional)
Small plastic drinks bottle or plastic vitamin bottle (optional)

Show your child how to peel the sticker off the backing and press it to a piece of paper. To make a wall hanging, press stickers to a paper plate. Make a vase by decorating a small fizzy drink or plastic vitamin bottle. You can also colour on plain white labels to make your own stickers.

Artwork Display

Here's a way to display your child's artwork on the refrigerator without having to cover it up with magnets to keep it there!

Wooden ruler (12-, 18-, or 24-inch)
Magnet strip (same length as ruler)
Glue gun
Clothes pegs, spring-type (at least 2)

Glue the magnetic strip to the back of the wooden ruler. Glue spring-type clothes pegs to the front of the ruler so that the pins open downward. Use two clothes pegs for a 12-inch ruler, placing one at each end. You may want to use three or four clothes pegs for a longer ruler. Write your child's name with marker or glitter on the front of the ruler, or let your child decorate the ruler and clothes pegs with paint, glitter, pasta and so on. When dry, place the ruler on the refrigerator and clip on your child's artwork with the clothes pegs.

Fishy Beanbag

Your child will have as much fun helping you make this easy beanbag as she will playing with it.

Sock
Dried beans
Wool
Marker
Glue
Felt scraps (optional)

Fill a child-size sock about three-quarters full with dried beans. Tie tightly with wool to make a tail. Push in the toe of the sock to form the mouth and insert glue to hold the shape. Use a marker to draw eyes and gills, or you can cut eyes, gills and fins from scraps of felt and glue them to the sock. Use the fishy beanbag to play catch, or try to throw it in an empty laundry basket.

Footprint T-shirt

This makes a great gift for mums, dads and grandparents.

Fabric paint
Paintbrush
White T-shirt

Paint your child's feet and press them onto a white T-shirt. You can paint them different colours and press them randomly over the shirt, or use one colour and make a trail of footprints up the front and down the back of the shirt. Personalise the T-shirt even more with an iron-on photograph or a special message written in fabric paint.

Fishy Necklace

This makes a great seasonal activity, too. Instead of fish, cut holiday shapes such as hearts or shamrocks.

Uncooked tube-shaped pasta, dyed or painted in bright colours
Paper card
Hole punch
Shoelace (18 inches or longer)
Scissors

Cut 3-to 4-inch long fish shapes from various colours of paper card; punch a hole for an eye in each fish. Show your child how to string the painted or dyed pasta alternately with the fish shapes onto the shoelace; tie the ends together to make a necklace. (Instead of using tube-shaped pasta, you can use straws cut into 1½-inch lengths, but these will be more difficult for toddlers to string.)

Bookmark

Here's another great gift idea for grandparents. You can also use these bookmarks as unique thankyou cards for gifts your child has received.

Pencil for tracing

Paper

Scissors

Crayons, markers, stickers and glitter for decorating

Clear contact paper

Place your child's hand and arm on a piece of paper and trace around it. Cut the tracing out of paper and have your child decorate it with crayons, markers, stickers, glitter and so on. Be sure to write your child's name and age or date on the back. Cover with clear contact paper and use for a bookmark.

Bedtime Buddy

Roll of drawing paper

Pen or marker

Old sheet

Scissors

Sewing machine or needle and thread

Cotton batting

Fabric paint

Have your child lie down on a large piece of drawing paper and trace around her body. Cut out the outline and use it as a pattern to cut two body outlines out of an old sheet. Sew them together around the edges, right sides in, leaving enough of the edges unsewn to turn the right sides out. Turn, stuff with cotton batting and sew the hole closed. Decorate with fabric paint and dress in your child's clothes.

CHAPTER 11
Birthday and Holiday Activities

'Of course, parents don't have children because they want to be martyrs, or at least they shouldn't. They have them because they love children and want some of their very own. They also love children because they remember being loved so much by their parents in their childhood. Taking care of their children, seeing them grow and develop into fine people, gives most parents despite the hard work their greatest satisfaction in life.'

– Dr Benjamin Spock

Holiday celebrations provide an important break from the day-to-day routine for children and adults. Whether you're preparing for a major celebration such as Christmas or you're simply making green jelly for Saint Patrick's Day, the anticipation of a special day can lift your spirits and impart a sense of family tradition to your children.

While toddlers are too young to understand much of the significance of each holiday, you can still make the most of each occasion. Begin by talking to your child about the upcoming event. Read simple library books that explain the story of your tradition. Look at videotapes/DVDs or photo albums of past family celebrations. When the holiday actually arrives, refer to the books you have read or photos you have looked at to help your child make the connection between the story and the event.

Keep in mind that for toddlers, celebrations do not need to be lavish. Bake a special batch of biscuits, paint pictures in seasonal colours, or invite friends over for a simple lunch or teddy-bear tea. To get the most out of the holiday, try to be as routine as possible about your child's meals and naps.

This chapter will suggest many ideas for celebrating holidays with toddlers. Many of the activities break my own rule about simplicity – they're a little complex for most toddlers to do on their own. You'll need to assist and, at times, do part of the process yourself. This does limit the learning value for your child, so try to make these activities the exception rather than the rule. But sometimes it's okay to make or do something just because you want to, rather than wondering and worrying about what your child will learn from it. Toddlers will benefit when you let them do the things they're capable of doing, even if it means not doing everything by themselves.

Birthday Celebrations

Although parents usually emphasise birthdays, most toddlers do not get into birthdays in a really big way. For the first few years of life, a family dinner complete with birthday cake and candles is often sufficient for a birthday celebration. However, if you want to invite a few friends over for a party, keep the festivities simple:

- Put some playdough or simple craft materials out to occupy the children until all guests have arrived.
- If there are no other adults on hand, ask the children's parents (or at least one or two) to stay for the party. They'll be a big help to you when it's time to organise the children for food, games, or circle time.

- Serve a simple meal of sandwiches or hot dogs, vegetable sticks and juice or chocolate milk. If you plan the party for midmorning or afternoon, put out a fruit platter and juice or milk with the birthday cake.

- Most toddlers are too young to enjoy group games, but sitting in a circle singing songs or doing simple finger plays can be great fun.

- After an hour and a half or two hours of eating, singing, playing and opening gifts, most little guests will be ready to depart. Have your child say goodbye to the guests individually as they leave.

Although sending 'thank you' notes may be an old-fashioned custom, it's one I started with my children long before they could understand the concept and it's one I hope they will continue into adulthood. (Good manners and gratitude are never out of date.) Use a piece of your child's artwork as an original 'thank you' card. Write the message yourself and, if you like, enclose a photograph of your child with each card.

Birthday Memory Book

Paper card
Stapler
Stickers, glitter and photograph(s) for decorating
Clear contact paper (optional)
Birthday cards and memorabilia
Glue

Staple or sew together ten (or more) sheets of paper card to make a birthday memory book for your child. Decorate the front with your child's name, age, birthday date and so on. Add stickers, glitter and a photograph of the birthday child and cover with clear contact paper if you like. Inside the book, your child can glue his birthday cards and other reminders of his special day.

Party Tablecloth

You can use this idea to make custom tablecloths for birthdays, holidays and other special events. An older child may enjoy making a tablecloth with his friends at his next birthday party.

Large roll or sheets of plain newsprint
Paint, crayons, or markers
Clear vinyl tablecloth

Cut a length of paper the size of the table to be covered. Let your children draw on the paper with crayons, markers, or paints. You may want to add stickers, or you can glue pictures cut from magazines. When the masterpiece is complete, place it on the table and cover with a clear vinyl tablecloth.

Video Time Capsule

If you like this idea, you'll want to begin as early as possible – your child's first birthday would be the perfect time.

Video camera
Videotape/DVD

If you have access to a video camera, consider making a videotape/DVD of your child on each birthday throughout his childhood. Beginning with his first birthday (if you can), spend a couple of minutes taping him sitting, crawling, standing, walking, or doing whatever stage he happens to be in. If you like, show his room, his favourite toys and books and so on. As the years progress and your child becomes more vocal, ask him questions about his favourite foods, songs, activities, friends and so on. Ask your child what he is looking forward to over the year and what he expects life to be like next year on his birthday. When the segment is complete, put the tape away and don't tape on it until next year's birthday. If doing this for more than one child, use a different tape for each, but use the tape only for the time capsule. Years down the road you'll be able to watch your child grow up on his video time capsule.

Valentine's Day (14 February)

Valentine's Day is for celebrating love. Although no one is quite sure how Valentine's Day and its accompanying traditions started, most of us enjoy sharing cards, chocolates, hugs and kisses with those we love on this day.

Valentine celebrations for toddlers can be kept simple. Read a book about Valentine's Day several times in the days and weeks prior to 14 February. Make simple red, white and pink decorations to put up around the house. Bake and ice some heart-shaped biscuits to give to a friend or neighbour. On Valentine's Day, dress the whole family in red and put your heart-shaped biscuit cutter to work for toast, sandwiches, apples, cheese and finger jelly. A small party with a few friends can be a simple and fun way to celebrate this special day.

Jelly Painting

1 package red jelly
Water
Paper card
Paintbrush
Scissors

Mix jelly with a small amount of water to make a fairly thick, spreadable paste. Cut a heart shape from a piece of paper card and have your child paint the heart with the jelly. Let dry. This makes a delicious-smelling valentine card or picture for someone special.

Valentine Postcard

Heavy white paper or postcard
Paper doily
Red or pink paint
Paintbrush or sponge
Clear contact paper (optional)

Place a paper doily on one side of a blank postcard, or on a piece of heavy white paper folded to make a card. You can hold the doily in place with a small amount of tacky adhesive or a paper clip. Paint or sponge over the doily and onto the postcard beneath it. Remove the doily and let the postcard dry. Cover with clear contact paper to give it a finished look.

Valentine Fairy cakes

Use this idea to make heart-shaped fairy cakes for Valentine's Day.

Marbles (1 for each fairy cake)
Paper baking cups
Cake batter
Frosting
Sprinkles and other candy for decorating

Wash and dry enough marbles so there's one for each fairy cake you're making. Line a fairy cake tin with paper baking cups. Place one marble in each section between the side of the paper cup and the tin (the marbles mould the baking cups into heart shapes). Pour in the batter and bake according to the recipe. Cool and decorate with frosting, sprinkles, chocolate chips etc.

Edible Valentines

Crackers
Love heart sweets, cinnamon hearts, or other heart-shaped sweets
Frosting

Use frosting to glue heart-shaped sweets to crackers for a completely edible valentine.

Sweetheart Sandwiches

Bread slices
Softened cream cheese
Red food colouring
Heart-shaped biscuit cutters
Honey and/or cinnamon (optional)

Mix softened cream cheese with a drop or two of red food colouring. Add more food colouring, one drop at a time, if you want a darker colour. If you like, flavour the cream cheese with honey and/or cinnamon. Spread the coloured cream cheese on slices of bread. Use biscuit cutters to cut out heart-shaped sandwiches.

Valentine Biscuits

Rolled biscuit dough
Heart-shaped biscuit cutters
Pink icing
Sprinkles or other candy for decorating

Prepare a batch of rolled biscuit dough ahead of time. Let your toddler help with some of the simpler parts of the recipe. Roll the dough out and use a heart-shaped biscuit cutter to cut heart shapes from the dough. Bake as directed and let cool. Ice with pink icing and decorate with sprinkles or other candy.

Valentine Heart

Pink paper card
Scissors
Red and white liquid poster paint
Spoons
Small rolling pin (optional)

Cut out large heart shapes from paper card; fold in half, then open again. Have your child use a spoon to dribble red and white liquid poster paint onto the heart. Fold the heart up with the paint on the inside; your child can use his hand or a small rolling pin to press on the top of the folded heart. Open up the heart again to see the designs the paint has made. You can write on the unpainted side of the heart, or glue it onto another sheet of white or red paper card to make a pretty Valentine's Day card.

Saint Patrick's Day (17 March)

Saint Patrick's Day can help break up the monotony of the last days of winter. Dress in green and invite a few friends over for a small Saint Patrick's Day celebration. Make a something together and play a few simple games. Serve green food such as fairy cakes or sugar biscuits with green icing (or decorate them as a party activity). Colour white grape juice green with a drop or two of food colouring, or serve limeade. Wind up the day with your own Saint Patrick's Day parade either in your living room or outside if the weather is fine.

Potato Press Picture

Raw potato, cut in half
Shallow dish of green poster paint
Paper card

Dip the cut surface of the potato into the green paint and press onto the paper card. Remind your child to press the potato onto the paper gently. Repeat until the paper is covered with green shapes. Use as a Saint Patrick's Day card or picture.

Shamrock Rubbings

Sandpaper
Scissors
Crayons
Paper

Cut shamrock shapes out of sandpaper. Use different grains of sandpaper and cut the shamrocks in several different sizes. Tape the shamrocks to a table. Show your child how to place his paper over the shamrock and rub with the side of a crayon to get a Saint Patrick's Day design.

Shamrock Necklace

Green and white paper card
Scissors
Hole punch
Shoelaces, ribbon, or wool for stringing

Cut several sizes of shamrocks from green and white paper card. Punch a hole in the top of each shamrock. Give your child a shoelace (or length of ribbon, or wool with masking tape wrapped on each end) and show him how to string the shamrocks to make a Saint Patrick's Day necklace.

Easter (Date Varies)

As well as the religious celebration Easter is also a time to celebrate the coming of spring and all the delightful signs of new life that abound. Easter is a great time for family dinners and small get-togethers with friends. Decorate Easter eggs together or make a simple Easter craft project. Hold an Easter egg hunt outdoors or in, depending on the weather. Have an informal parade in your neighbourhood with decorated wagons and tricycles. This is another wonderful holiday that helps break the monotony of the last few days of winter, so start your Easter craft projects and activities early.

Easy Easter Eggs

These Easter eggs are easy enough for even the littlest hands to make.

> *Cotton swabs*
> *Cotton balls*
> *Liquid poster paint*
> *Hard-boiled eggs*
> *Clear acrylic spray (optional)*

Dip a cotton swab or cotton ball in paint and use to dab paint on the hard-boiled egg. For a shiny finish, spray with clear acrylic spray.

Easter Bouquet

Paper baking cups
Scissors
Pipe cleaners
Glue
Ribbon
Glitter

Poke a hole with scissors or a pen through the bottom of the baking cup. Stick a pipe cleaner through the hole. Bend the top of the pipe cleaner over and glue into place. Spread glue over the paper baking cup and decorate with glitter. Bunch together four or five flowers, twisting the pipe cleaner stems together. Tie with ribbon to make a spring-time bouquet.

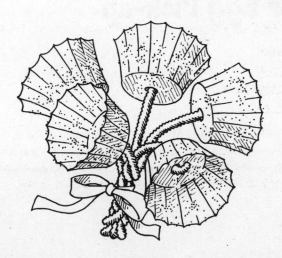

Tissue Paper Eggs

Coloured tissue paper
White craft glue
Hard-boiled eggs
Clear acrylic spray (optional)

Tear coloured tissue paper into small pieces. Dilute white craft glue with a few drops of water. Have your child spread glue on the hard-boiled egg with his fingers. After he has washed his hands, show him how to gently press pieces of tissue paper onto the egg. Cover with a light coating of glue or spray with clear acrylic spray.

Easter Egg Pick-up

Tissue paper
Pie plate
Plastic drinking straws
Scissors

Cut several tissue paper eggs about three inches long. Place the eggs in a pie plate. Show your child how to put the straw to his mouth and take a deep breath, seeing how many eggs he can pick up on the end of the straw.

Easter Egg Holder

This is an easy way to display all the eggs your child decorates.

Empty paper towel roll
Scissors
Paper card
Glue
Glitter or stickers for decorating

Cut the paper towel roll into 2-inch sections. Cut strips of paper card 2 inches wide and long enough to wrap around the paper towel roll. Glue the paper card strips to the pieces of paper towel roll and decorate with glitter or stickers.

Tissue Easter Egg

Coloured tissue paper cut into 3-inch squares
Paper card
Scissors
Glue

Cut an egg shape from a piece of paper card. Show your child how to wad the tissue paper square, dip it in glue and stick it to the egg.

Easter Egg Necklace

Paper card in several different colours
Scissors
Hole punch
Shoelace, ribbon or wool
Glue, glitter, sequins or stickers (optional)

Cut out some egg-shaped pieces of paper card in several different colours. Punch a hole in the top of each egg. If you like, decorate with crayons, markers, stickers, glitter, or sequins. Show your child how to slip the end of the shoelace through the holes in the eggs to make a necklace. You'll need to tie something temporarily onto one end of the shoelace to make sure the eggs don't fall off the other end as he adds them. If using ribbon or wool, taping the end makes it easier for little fingers to thread it through the hole.

Halloween (31 October)

Halloween began in ancient times as a pagan celebration of the arrival of winter. It was then that the Lord of Death called together all the souls of the wicked who had died during the past year. The Druids believed that on this night ghosts, goblins and witches would appear and harm people. Huge bonfires and masks were meant to frighten away these evil beings. People dressed in costumes of animal skins so that the spirits wouldn't recognise them. Special food left on the doorstep to appease the spirits began the tradition of trick-or-treating.

Despite its frightening origins, Halloween has become a fun tradition for many people – adults and children alike. As with most other holidays, toddlers are too young to understand the significance of Halloween. They can, however, be easily frightened by some of the activities which surround this day, so it's wise to be careful where you take them at this time of year.

Churches and community centres often have autumn carnivals or parties where children can play games, eat food and have fun without the dangers associated with trick-or-treating. If you want to have a small Halloween party yourself, encourage friends to dress in fun, non-scary costumes. Make a simple craft project, then decorate and eat some Halloween biscuits, fairy cakes, or other treats.

Regardless of how you celebrate this occasion, here are some fun activities for you and your child to do together.

Painted Spider Web

White poster paint
Black paper card
Drinking straw

Drop a bit of thin white poster paint onto the centre of a piece of black paper card. Give your child a straw and show him how to blow the paint around to make a spider web.

Pumpkin Prints

Very small pumpkin
Knife
Orange and black poster paint
Paper

Cut a small pumpkin in half and dip it into orange and black paint. Press it onto paper to make a pumpkin print. When the paint dries, cover with clear contact paper for a Halloween place mat, or fold the paper in half to make a Halloween card.

Paper Plate Spider Web

Even if you're not into spiders at Halloween, this is a neat idea for any time of the year.

Paper plate
Pie plate or round cake tin
Black paint
Marble

Place a paper plate inside a metal or aluminium pie plate or round cake pan. Put a small amount of black paint in the centre of the paper plate and drop a marble in. Your child will have fun moving and tilting the pie plate or cake pan from side to side to make a spider web on his plate.

For a variation, paint the paper plate dark blue or black first and use white paint for a more realistic looking spider web, or use more than one colour of paint for a rainbow spider web.

Jack-o'-Orange

Orange
Whole cloves
Black marker

Use a black marker to draw a simple face on an orange. Show your child how to poke the cloves into the orange to make a Halloween face.

Paper Bag Pumpkin

Paper bag
Newspaper or other paper for crumpling
Twist tie, rubber band, or string
Orange and green poster paint
Paintbrush
Black marker

Crumple up newspaper or other scraps of paper and stuff the bag until it is about two-thirds full. Close the bag with a twist tie, rubber band, or piece of string. Twist the unstuffed part of the bag to make a stem. Paint the pumpkin part of the bag orange and paint the stem green. When the paint is dry, draw a face on the pumpkin with a black marker.

Christmas (25 December)

Christmas is a time when Christians the world over celebrate the birth of Jesus Christ. For some, Christmas means the arrival of Santa Claus, Father Christmas or Saint Nicholas. Christmas celebrations usually emphasise family togetherness, doing thoughtful and loving things for others and lots of good food.

However Christmas is celebrated, most will agree that this time of year often brings with it more than peace, joy, love and goodwill. For adults, Christmas often means a time of frenzied activity, extra stress and financial demands that can be hard to meet. Sometimes unrealistic expectations – those we have of ourselves, those we have of others and those others have of us – make it hard to truly enjoy the wonders of the season.

At this busy time of year, concentrate on what is important. Spend your time, money and energy on activities that will build or uphold family traditions and make memories for your child. Don't forget simple pleasures like reading together, singing carols by the Christmas tree, or making a holiday craft. Bake some Christmas biscuits together, go for a walk in the snow and sip hot chocolate by the fire. Children need your time and attention more than anything else. Although your child may soon forget toys and other material things, time spent together makes memories he will treasure for a lifetime.

Some of these activities may be too complex for some toddlers. Remember to allow your child to do the parts he is capable of doing. Simple painting projects or tissue paper collages in seasonal colours are also great Christmas activities for toddlers.

Cinnamon Drawing

Sandpaper
Scissors
Cinnamon sticks

Cut the sandpaper into a holiday shape such as a star, Christmas tree, or gingerbread man. Show your child how to rub the cinnamon stick on the sandpaper to make both a nice design and a pleasing fragrance. If you like, punch a hole at the top of the sandpaper and string wool through it to make a Christmas tree decoration.

Animal Dressing up

Stuffed animals or dolls
Christmas ribbon, bows or fabric

When decorating your home for the holidays, encourage your child to do some decorating of his own. Dress up your child's favourite dolls or stuffed animals with some Christmas ribbon or big bright bows or use Christmas fabric to create scarves or kerchiefs. Display the animals on a shelf in your child's room or on a mantel in a more prominent part of your house.

Cotton Ball Snowman

Cotton balls
Clear contact paper
Paper card
Scissors
Stapler

Cut three circles from clear contact paper. The circles should be in three different sizes ranging from a diameter of 1½–2 inches to 4½–5 inches. Staple the contact paper, backing side up, to the paper card to form a snowman shape. Your child can peel off the backing and stick cotton balls to the contact paper to cover the snowman. If you like, cut additional snowman features such as a hat or carrot from paper card and glue to the snowman.

Christmas Tree

Lids from jars (at least 10)
Magnet strips
Glue gun
Green felt
Felt in other bright colours
Scissors

Cut small circles of coloured felt to fit the lids. Use lots of green and other colours such as red, yellow and blue. Glue a small magnetic strip to the other side of each lid. You can arrange these magnets in the shape of a Christmas tree on your refrigerator door. Your toddler will have fun making designs of his own.

Pencil Holder

Tape and toddlers are a great combination. Your child will have fun making this pencil holder (or vase) as a Christmas gift for a family member or friend.

> *Small, clean can*
> *Masking tape*
> *Brown liquid shoe polish or poster paint*
> *Clear acrylic spray or shellac*

Show your toddler how to tear small pieces of masking tape and stick them onto a small can. If your toddler has trouble tearing the tape, tear the tape for him and place the pieces around the rim of an upside-down tuna can or plastic container. When the can is covered with pieces of masking tape, paint with brown liquid shoe polish or poster paint to create a leathery look. If brown isn't high on your child's list of favourite colours, choose another colour. When the paint or shoe polish is dry, spray with clear acrylic spray, or brush with shellac to give the pencil holder a shiny finish.

Rudolph Sandwiches

Sliced bread
Peanut butter
Pretzels
Raisins
Cherry

Cut a slice of bread into a triangle shape. Spread the triangle of bread with peanut butter (or use jam, honey, or cream cheese according to your child's preference). Add pretzels for antlers, raisins for eyes and a bright red cherry for Rudolph's nose.

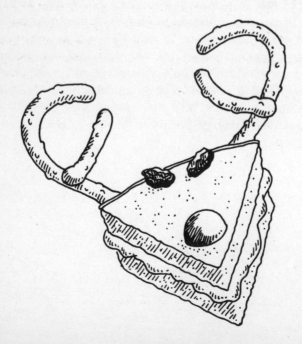

Christmas Bag

Your child can use this bag to wrap a gift in, or you can have one on hand for each member of the family on Christmas morning. It will help keep cards and small, opened gifts from getting lost in the sea of boxes, wrapping and presents.

> *Large paper bag*
> *Glue*
> *Bits of wrapping paper, stickers, ribbon fabric and Christmas cards*

Spread glue on one side of a large paper bag. Let your child stick whatever materials you have handy on the bag: small pieces of wrapping paper, seasonal stickers, ribbon, fabric, or pictures cut from old Christmas cards. If you like, decorate the other side of the bag in the same way.

Smelly Christmas Tree

Paper card
Scissors
Glue
One package green jelly
Empty salt shaker or spice container
Paintbrush
Hole punch (optional)
Ribbon or string (optional)

Cut a Christmas tree shape from a piece of paper card. Use the paintbrush to spread glue all over the tree. Sprinkle jelly powder onto the glue. Shake off excess jelly and allow to dry.

Use as a Christmas card or punch a hole in the top of the tree, insert a loop of ribbon or string through the hole and use as a Christmas tree ornament.

Gingerbread Men

1 cup shortening

¾ cup honey

1 egg

1 cup molasses

1½ teaspoon baking soda

½ teaspoon salt

2 teaspoons ground ginger

1 teaspoon cinnamon

1 teaspoon ground cloves

5 cups flour

Raisins, nuts, licorice and small sweets for decorating

Mix shortening, honey, egg and molasses. Sift soda, salt, ginger, cinnamon, cloves and flour together. Mix wet and dry ingredients. Refrigerate dough until cold. Roll out chilled dough ¼ inch thick on a floured surface. Cut with a gingerbread men biscuit cutter. Decorate with raisins, nuts, licorice and other small candies. Bake at 190C/375F/ Gas mark 5 for 10 minutes.

If you like, bake the gingerbread men ahead of time and let your child decorate the cooled biscuits with icing and small sweets. If your family isn't fond of gingerbread, don't let that stop you. Substitute another rolled biscuit dough recipe instead.

Stone Paperweight

This paperweight is easy for toddlers to make and a great Christmas gift for someone special.

Large, smooth stone
Poster paint
Paintbrush
Shellac
Glitter (optional)

Go on a walk with your toddler and look for a large, smooth stone. At home, have your child paint the stone in his favourite colours. When dry, brush with shellac for a shiny finish. If you like, sprinkle glitter on the shellac before it dries.

Krispie Christmas Treats

5 cups Rice Krispies
¼ cup butter or margarine
4 cups mini-marshmallows (or 40 large marshmallows)
Red or green food colouring
Metal biscuit cutters in Christmas shapes

Melt margarine in a saucepan, then add marshmallows and cook over low heat, stirring constantly until syrupy. Add food colouring and stir until the colour is well mixed in. Remove from heat, add cereal and stir until well coated. Press into a baking tray and let cool. Use metal Christmas-shaped biscuit cutters to cut out some Christmas treats.

Christmas Doorknob Decoration

Red felt
Plastic lid for tracing, about 4 inches in diameter
Green felt
Glue Stickers, glitter, beads, sequins and so on

Cut a 4-inch circle out of red felt. Cut out a 1inch circle in the middle of the red circle and cut four ½-inch slits outward from the inner circle to allow it to fit over a doorknob. Cut a 7-inch Christmas tree shape from the green felt. Glue the top of the tree to the bottom of the red felt circle. Your child can decorate his tree with beads, glitter, sequins, stickers, or any other scraps you have on hand.

Appendix A

Basic Craft Recipes

Although your toddler is still quite young, she is already beginning to develop creative skills. She undoubtedly loves to scribble on paper (or walls) and already may have experienced the joy of finger-painting. You have probably noticed that she doesn't care as much for what she makes as for the process of working with materials of different colours and textures. Whether it's the process or the product that interests your child, the craft materials in this appendix are essential for her artwork. On the following pages you'll find easy recipes for paint, glue, paste, modelling compounds and more.

PAINT

Each of these nine recipes will produce a good quality paint for your child's use. The ingredients and preparation vary from recipe to recipe, so choose one that best suits the supplies and time you have available.

When mixing paint, keep in mind the age of your young artist. As a general rule, younger children require thicker paint and brushes. Paint should always be stored in covered containers. Small plastic spill-proof paint containers are available at art supply shops. Each comes with an airtight lid, holds brushes upright without tipping and is well worth the purchase price of several euro.

Flour-Based Poster Paint

¼ cup flour
1 cup water
Small jars or plastic containers
3 tablespoons powdered poster paint per container
2 tablespoons water per container
½ teaspoon liquid starch or liquid detergent per container

Measure flour into saucepan. Slowly add 1 cup water while stirring to make a smooth paste. Heat, stirring constantly, until paste begins to thicken. Cool. Measure ¼ cup paste into each small container. Add 3 tablespoons powdered poster paint and 2 tablespoons water to each container. For a matte finish, add liquid starch. For a glossy finish, add liquid detergent. Store covered.

Washing-Up Liquid Poster Paint

Small jars or plastic containers
1 tablespoon clear washing up liquid per container
2 teaspoons powdered poster paint per container

In each small container, mix together 1 tablespoon washing up liquid and 2 teaspoons powdered poster paint. This recipe makes enough for one painting session.

Cornflour Paint

Medium saucepan
½ cup cornflour
½ cup cold water
4 cups boiling water
Small jars or plastic containers
Poster paint, dry or liquid

Measure cornflour into saucepan. Add cold water to cornflour and stir to make a smooth paste. Stir in boiling water.

Place saucepan over medium to low heat and stir until boiling. Boil for 1 minute; remove from heat. Cool. Spoon about ½ cup of thickened cornflour mixture into each container, using a different cup for each colour. For each colour, stir 1 teaspoon dry poster or 1 tablespoon liquid poster into cornflour mixture. (Use more paint for more intense colour.) If paint is too thick, stir in 1 teaspoon water at a time until desired consistency is achieved. Store in refrigerator. This recipe makes about 4 cups of paint.

Condensed Milk Paint

Bowl
1 cup condensed milk
Food colouring

In bowl, mix 1 cup condensed milk with many drops of food colouring to make a very bright, glossy paint. This paint is not intended to be eaten, but it won't harm a child who decides to make a snack of it. Store covered in refrigerator.

Homemade Face Paint

Small jars or plastic containers
1 teaspoon cornflour per container
½ teaspoon cream per container
½ teaspoon water per container
Food colouring

In each small container, mix cornflour and cream until well blended. Add water and stir. Add food colouring one drop at a time until you get the desired colour. Paint small designs on face with a small paintbrush; remove with soap and water. Store covered.

Edible Egg-Yolk Paint

Small jars or plastic containers
1 egg yolk per container
¼ teaspoon water per container
Food colouring

In each small container, mix one egg yolk with ¼ teaspoon water and many drops of food colouring. Use a paintbrush to apply paint to freshly baked biscuits; return biscuits to oven until paint hardens.

Cornflour Finger-paint

3 tablespoons sugar
½ cup cornflour
Medium saucepan
2 cups cold water
Fairy cake tin or small cups
Food colouring
Soap flakes or washing up liquid

Mix sugar and cornflour in saucepan. Turn heat on low, add cold water and stir until mixture is thick. Remove from heat. Divide mixture into four or five portions, spooning into fairy cake tin sections or small cups. Add a few drops of food colouring and a pinch of soap flakes or a drop of washing up liquid to each portion. Stir and allow to cool before use. Store covered.

Flour Finger-paint

1 cup flour
2 tablespoons salt
Saucepan
1½ cups cold water
Wire whisk or eggbeater
1¼ cups hot water
Food colouring or poster paint

Put flour and salt in saucepan. Add cold water and beat with whisk or eggbeater until smooth. Add hot water and boil until mixture is thick. Beat again until smooth. Colour as desired with food colouring or powdered poster paint. Store covered in refrigerator.

PLAYDOUGH

Everyone seems to have a favourite playdough recipe and many old favourites have been included here. Some require cooking and some don't; some are meant to be eaten and some are not. Choose the recipe that best suits your needs and the ingredients you have on hand. Store playdough in a covered container or Ziploc bag. If it sweats a little, just add more flour. For sensory variety, use playdough warm or cool as well as at room temperature.

Porridge Playdough

1 part flour
1 part water
2 parts porridge oats
Bowl

Combine all ingredients in a bowl; mix well and knead until smooth. This playdough is not intended to be eaten, but it will not hurt a child who decides to taste it. Store covered in refrigerator. Your child can make this playdough without help; however, it doesn't last as long as cooked playdough.

Uncooked Playdough

Bowl
1 cup cold water
1 cup salt
2 teaspoons vegetable oil
Poster paint or food colouring
3 cups flour
2 tablespoons cornflour

In bowl, mix water, salt, oil and enough poster paint or food colouring to make a bright colour. Gradually add flour and cornflour until the mixture reaches the consistency of bread dough. Store covered.

Salt Playdough

1 cup salt
1 cup water
½ cup flour plus additional flour
Saucepan

Mix salt, water and flour in saucepan and cook over medium heat. Remove from heat when mixture is thick and rubbery. As the mixture cools, knead in enough flour to make the dough workable.

Coloured Playdough

1 cup water
1 tablespoon vegetable oil
½ cup salt
1 tablespoon cream of tartar
Food colouring
Saucepan
1 cup flour

Combine water, oil, salt, cream of tartar and food colouring in a saucepan and heat until warm. Remove from heat and add flour. Stir, then knead until smooth. The cream of tartar makes this dough last 6 months or longer, so resist the temptation to omit this ingredient if you don't have it on hand. Store this dough in an airtight container or a Ziploc freezer bag.

CLAY

Use the following recipes to make clay that can be rolled or shaped into sculptures. Some clays should be dried overnight, while others are best baked in an oven. When hard, sculptures can be decorated and preserved with acrylic paint to finish.

Modelling Clay

2 cups salt
⅔ cups water
Saucepan
1 cup cornflour
½ cup cold water

Stir salt and water in a saucepan over heat for 4-5 minutes. Remove from heat; add cornflour and cold water. Stir until smooth; return to heat and cook until thick. Allow the clay to cool, then shape as desired. When dry, decorate with paint, markers, glitter and so on. If you like, finish with clear acrylic spray or clear nail polish. Store unused clay in a Ziploc bag.

Bread Clay

6 slices white bread, crusts removed
6 tablespoons white glue
½ teaspoon detergent or 2 teaspoons glycerine
Food colouring
Paintbrush
Equal parts white glue and water
Acrylic paint or spray or clear nail polish

Knead bread with glue plus detergent or glycerine until the mixture is no longer sticky. Separate into portions and tint with food colouring. Let your child shape the clay. Brush the sculpture with equal parts glue and water for a smooth appearance. Let dry overnight. Use acrylic paints or spray or clear nail polish to seal and preserve.

Baker's Clay

4 cups flour
1 cup salt
1 teaspoon alum
1½ cups water
Food colouring (optional)
Large bowl
Biscuit cutters, drinking straw and fine wire (optional)
Baking sheet
Fine sandpaper
Plastic-based poster paint, acrylic paint, or markers
Clear varnish, acrylic spray, or nail polish

Mix flour, salt, alum and water in bowl. If dough is too dry, knead in another tablespoon of water. Dough can be coloured by dividing it into several parts and kneading a few drops of food colouring into each part. Roll or mould into ornaments.

To roll: Roll dough 1/8 inch thick on a lightly floured surface. Cut with biscuit cutters dipped in flour. Make a hole for hanging by dipping the end of a drinking straw in flour and using the straw to cut a tiny circle ¼ inch from the ornament's edge. You can also use the straw to cut more clay dots for use as decorations.

To mould: Shape dough into figures such as flowers, fruits, animals and so on. The figures should be no more than ½ inch thick. Insert fine wire in ornaments for hanging. Bake ornaments on an ungreased baking sheet for about 30 minutes at 130C/250F/Gas mark 1. Turn and bake another 90 minutes until hard and dry. Remove from oven and cool, then smooth with fine sandpaper. Decorate both sides of ornaments with plastic-based poster paint, acrylic paint, or markers. Let dry and seal with clear varnish, acrylic spray, or nail polish.

Makes about five dozen 2½-inch ornaments.

No-Bake Craft Clay

1 cup cornflour
1¼ cups cold water
2 cups baking soda (1 pound)
Saucepan
Food colouring (optional)
Plate
Damp cloth
Poster or acrylic paints (optional)
Clear varnish, acrylic spray, or nail polish

Combine cornflour, water and baking soda in saucepan; stir over medium heat for about 4 minutes until mixture thickens to a moist mashed potato consistency. (For coloured clay, add a few drops of food colouring to the water before it is mixed with cornflour and baking soda.) Remove from heat, turn onto plate and cover with a damp cloth until cool. Knead until smooth. Shape as desired or store in an airtight container or Ziploc bag. Dry sculptures overnight, then paint with poster paint or acrylic. Seal with varnish, acrylic spray, or nail polish.

No-Bake Biscuit Clay

2 cups salt
⅔ cup water
Medium saucepan
1 cup cornflour
½ cup cold water
Rolling pin
Biscuit cutters
Drinking straw
Paint, glitter and other decorative materials

Mix salt with ⅔ cup water in saucepan. Stir and boil until salt dissolves. Remove from heat. Add cornflour and ½ cup cold water and stir. If mixture doesn't immediately thicken, heat and stir until it does. Sprinkle cornflour on table and rolling pin. Roll out clay and cut with biscuit cutters. Use straw to make holes for hanging. Let dry overnight and decorate with paint, glitter and so on. Remind your child that these ornaments are not edible!

GLUE AND PASTE

The following glue and paste recipes use a variety of ingredients and methods. Choose the one that best suits your project. For variety, add food colouring before using. Store all glues and pastes in airtight containers in the refrigerator.

Glue
¾ cup water
2 tablespoons golden syrup
1 teaspoon white vinegar
Small saucepan
Small bowl
2 tablespoons cornflour
¾ cup cold water

Mix water, golden syrup and vinegar in saucepan. Bring to a full boil. In bowl, mix cornflour with cold water. Add this mixture slowly to the hot mixture, stirring constantly until the mixture returns to a boil. Boil for 1 minute, then remove from heat. When cooled, pour into another container and let stand overnight before using.

Homemade Paste

½ cup flour
Cold water
Saucepan
Food colouring (optional)

Add cold water to flour until mixture is as thick as whipped cream. Simmer and stir in saucepan for 5 minutes. Add a few drops of food colouring, if desired. This wet, messy paste takes a while to dry.

Papier-Maché Paste

1 cup water
¼ cup flour
5 cups lightly boiling water
Large saucepan

Mix flour into 1 cup water until mixture is thin and runny. Stir this mixture into lightly boiling water. Gently boil and stir 2 – 3 minutes. Cool before using.

No-Cook Paste

Bowl
½ cup flour
Water
Salt

In a bowl, mix flour with enough water to make a mixture that's gooey, but not runny. Add a pinch of salt; stir.

DECORATIONS

Use the following recipes to make decorative materials for use in various art and craft projects.

Colourful Creative Salt

½ cup salt
5-6 drops food colouring
Microwave and microwave-safe container or wax paper

Add food colouring to salt and stir well. Cook in microwave 1-2 minutes or spread on wax paper and let dry. Store in airtight container. Use as glitter.

Pasta Dye

½ cup rubbing alcohol
Food colouring
Dry pasta
Newspaper
Wax paper

Mix alcohol and food colouring in a bowl. Add small amounts of dry pasta to the liquid and gently mix. The larger the pasta, the longer it will take to absorb the colour. Dry on newspapers covered with wax paper. Remind your child that pasta dyed with this recipe is not for eating; it's only for art projects!

Egg Dye

Small bowls or cups
¼ teaspoon food colouring per container
¾ cup hot water per container
1 tablespoon white vinegar per container

Measure all liquids into bowl or cup and mix. Use a different colour in each container. Soak eggs in dye until they reach the desired shades.

Ornamental Frosting

3 egg whites
1 teaspoon cream of tartar
Bowl
Eggbeater
1 pound powdered sugar (about 4 cups), sifted
Damp cloth

Beat egg whites with cream of tartar in bowl until stiff peaks form. Add sugar and continue beating until mixture is thick and holds its shape. Cover bowl with damp cloth when not in use. This frosting can be made from several hours to a day before use. It makes a great glue for gingerbread houses and other edible works of art. Store in an airtight container in the refrigerator.

Appendix B

Crazy Can Activities

The following activities are suitable for a toddler Crazy Can (see Chapter 1). These activities require no special materials or time-consuming preparation or cleaning up and they need only a minimal amount of adult participation. Some of these activities require a little advance planning, such as having a collection of nuts and bolts on hand for Nuts and Bolts or preparing a craft carton for Cartons of Fun. A Crazy Can will provide you with an instant remedy when things start to get crazy or when there's just 'nothing to do'. (The number following each activity refers to the page on which it is found.)

- Bottles and Lids, 39
- Cartons of Fun, 64
- Chair Maze, 36
- Peg Tin, 45
- Clothes Peg Poke, 49
- Felt Faces, 146
- Fun with Balls, 74
- Fun with Tissues, 54
- Fun with Tape, 43
- Ice Cube Bags, 40
- Jingle Bell Bracelet, 197
- Postbox, 42
- No-Cook Squishy Bag, 68
- Nuts and Bolts, 54
- Painting Bag, 69
- Hedgehog Playdough, 59
- Ring Fun, 47
- Sandpaper Play, 147
- Stacking Fun, 77
- Sticky Feet, 38
- Threading, 44

Appendix C

Best Toys for Babies and Toddlers

If your child is less than one year old, she probably has not yet amassed a big collection of toys. After a few birthdays and Christmas celebrations, however, she will likely have more toys than you ever dreamed possible! It's a good idea to think ahead about the kinds of toys you want to invest in. There are a lot of toys out there and more are coming out all the time. Some are worth the money they cost, while others definitely aren't.

When choosing toys for children, look for items that can be used in more than one way, that have stood the test of time and that may be enjoyed through many years of childhood. The toys listed in this appendix meet all these criteria and are worth every penny.

For storage, try to stay away from toy boxes, which take up a lot of space and aren't particularly useful for organizing. (We have two toy boxes, lovingly handmade by Grandpa, that we use for stuffed animals and dressing-up clothes.) Store items with many pieces in stackable, transparent plastic containers with lids. These fit well in closets or on shelves. Flat containers are also practical, as they slide easily under beds, utilising otherwise wasted space. Storing toys in smaller containers instead of a toy box keeps pieces from getting mixed up (provided you don't allow your child to take out all the containers at once) and helps children develop organisational skills.

Other ideas for making the best use of toys include establishing a toy rotation or implementing a toy exchange with friends. See Chapter 1 for details.

The book *What to Expect the Toddler Years* by Arlene Eisenberg, Heidi E. Markoff and Sandee E. Hathaway includes a great list called 'Toys for Tots Early in the Second Year.' The list is organised according to skills the toys help develop. Most of our family favourites are included in this list, so I have organised my recommendations in somewhat the same way. Many toys help develop more than one skill, but for simplicity's sake, I have avoided duplications.

Toys that help build fine motor skills (many also encourage discovery and interest in the physical world):

beads	sandbox and	spools
blocks	sand toys	stacking toys
boxes	shape sorters	water toys
containers	simple wooden	
nesting toys	jigsaw puzzles	

Toys that help build gross motor skills:

balls	push toys	slides
pull toys	riding toys	swings

Toys that stimulate imagination (many also encourage learning about the grown-up world):

books	fake food	tea sets
building toys	kitchen accessories	toy cars
doll furniture	puppets	toy telephones
dolls	shopping carts	
dressing up clothes	stuffed animals	

Toys that stimulate creativity (basic craft supplies):

child-safe scissors	glue	markers paper
colouring books	paint	playdough
crayons	paintbrushes	sponges

Toys that encourage musical play:

cassette tapes	tambourines	xylophones
drums	simple keyboards	
maracas	sturdy cassette player	

Appendix D

Resources

Very few ideas in this world are truly original; that is, no matter how new or unique an idea may seem, someone somewhere has probably had it before. Many of the ideas in this book have appeared in print elsewhere and many of them you have probably seen, heard about, or tried yourself. I have included in this book only the very best ideas for toddlers – the ones that are the most fun as well as the most practical. These ideas were gleaned from a combination of personal experience, contributions from friends and family and information gathered from the books listed below.

Catlin, Cynthia. *Toddlers Together: The Complete Planning Guide for a Toddler Curriculum.* Beltsville, MD: Gryphon House, 1994.

Charner, Kathy, ed. *The Giant Encyclopedia of Theme Activities for Children 2 to 5.* Beltsville, MD: Gryphon House, 1993.

Dexter, Sandi. *Joyful Play with Toddlers: Recipes for Fun with Odds and Ends.* Seattle: Parenting Press, 1995.

Eisenberg, Arlene, Heidi E. Markoff and Sandee E. Hathaway. *What to Expect the Toddler Years.* New York: Workman Publishing Company, 1994.

Ellison, Sheila, and Judith Gray. *365 Days of Baby Love: Playing, Growing and Exploring with Babies from Birth to Age 2.* Naperville, IL: Sourcebooks, 1996.

Ellison, Sheila, and Judith Gray. *365 Days of Creative Play: For Children Two Years and Up.* Naperville, IL: Sourcebooks, 1995.

Ellison, Sheila, and Judith Gray. *365 Foods Kids Love to Eat*. Naperville, IL: Sourcebooks, 1995.

Gilbert, Labritta. *Do Touch: Instant, Easy Hands-On Learning Experiences for Young Children*. Beltsville, MD: Gryphon House, 1989.

Haas, Carolyn Buhai. *Look at Me: Creative Learning Activities for Babies and Toddlers*. Chicago: Chicago Review Press, 1987.

Hunt, Gladys. *Honey for a Child's Heart: The Imaginative Use of Books in Family Life*. 3rd ed. Grand Rapids, MI: Zondervan Publishing House, 1989.

Jones, Claudia. *Parents are Teachers, Too: Enriching Your Child's First Six Years*. Charlotte, VT: Williamson Publishing Company, 1988.

Jones, Maggie. *Understanding Your Child through Play*. Toronto: Stoddart Publishing Company, 1989.

Kohl, Mary Ann F. *Preschool Art: It's the Process, Not the Product*. Beltsville, MD: Gryphon House, 1994.

Landsberg, Michele. *Reading for the Love of It: Best Books for Young Readers*. Upper Saddle River, NJ: Prentice Hall, 1987.

Lansky, Vicky. *Feed Me! I'm Yours*. Minnetonka, MN: Meadowbrook Press, 1974.

Leach, Penelope. *Your Baby and Child: From Birth to Age Five*. New York: Alfred A. Knopf, 1990.

Martin, Elaine. *The Baby Games: The Joyful Guide to Child's Play from Birth to Three Years*. Toronto: Stoddart Publishing Company, 1988.

Matterson, Elizabeth. *Games for the Very Young*. American Heritage Press, New York: 1969.

Mayesky, Mary. *Creative Activities for Young Children*. 4th ed. Albany: Delmar Publishers, 1990.

Miller, Karen. *More Things to Do with Toddlers and Twos*. Chelsea, MA: Telshare Publishing, 1990.

Miller, Karen. *Things to Do with Toddlers and Twos*. Chelsea, MA: Telshare Publishing, 1984.

Pfiffners, George. *Earth-Friendly Toys: How to Make Fabulous Toys and Games from Reusable Objects*. John Wiley and Sons, 1994.

Reitzes, Fretta, and Beth Teitelman. *Wonderplay: Interactive and Developmental Games, Crafts, and Creative Activities for Infants, Toddlers, and Preschoolers*. Philadelphia: Running Press, 1995.

Rossi, Mary Jane Mangini. *Read to Me! Teach Me!* Wauwatosa, WI: American Baby Books, 1982.

Silberg, Jackie. *Games to Play with Toddlers*. Beltsville, MD: Gryphon House, 1993.

Silberg, Jackie. *Games to Play with Two Year Olds*. Beltsville, MD: Gryphon House, 1994.

Spencer, Zane. *One Hundred Fifty Plus! Games and Activities for Early Childhood*. Belmont, CA: Lake Publishers, 1976.

Suid, Anna. *Holiday Crafts*. Palo Alto, CA: Monday Morning Books, 1985.

Trelease, Jim. *The Read-Aloud Handbook*. 4th ed. New York: Penguin Books, 1995.

Warren, Jean. *1-2-3 Art*. Everett, WA: Warren Publishing House, 1985.

Zaslavsky, Claudia. *Preparing Young Children for Math*. New York: Schocken Books, 1979.

Index

D

E

MERCIER PRESS
WHAT YOU NEED TO READ

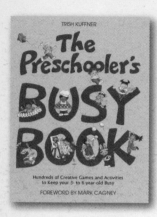

The Preschooler's Busy Book

Hundreds of Creative Games and Activities to Keep your 3- to 6-year-old Busy

Trish Kuffner
Foreword by Mark Cagney

ISBN: 1 85635 502 0

The Preschooler's Busy Book by (blessed) Trish Kuffner,
HUNDREDS OF CREATIVE GAMES AND ACTIVITIES TO KEEP YOUR
3- TO 6-YEAR-OLD BUSY... as essential as a first aid kit. It nearly made me want
another child, it's that good!!!!!

Mark Cagney

The Preschooler's Busy Book shows parents how to entertain their three- to six-year-olds using items found around the home. It shows parents and day-care providers how to:

✐ Prevent boredom during even the longest stretches of indoor weather with ideas for indoor play, kitchen activities, and arts and crafts projects.

✐ Encourage a child's physical, mental and emotional growth with ideas for music, dance, drama and outdoor play.

✐ Celebrate holidays and other occasions with special projects and activities.

✐ Keep children occupied during long trips or short car journeys.

The Preschooler's Busy Book is written with warmth and sprinkled with humour and insight. It should be required reading for anyone raising or teaching preschool-age children.